Introduction to Christian Evidences

by Heath Rogers

ONE STONE
BIBLICAL RESOURCES

Published by:
One Stone Press
979 Lovers Lane
Bowling Green, KY 42103

Printed in the United States of America

ISBN 10: 1-941422-20-9
ISBN 13: 978-1-941422-20-5

ONE STONE
BIBLICAL RESOURCES

www.onestone.com

Introduction

Young people have to develop their own faith. Not only do they need their own convictions regarding things like God and the Bible, they need to know why they have these convictions. Sooner or later, young believers will encounter things that will cause them to question their faith. Perhaps it's a tragedy that causes them to doubt God. Maybe it's a friend or adult who belittles their faith. The constant bombardment of evolution being taught as fact can certainly have an impact on one's thinking. If a Christian doesn't know why they believe what they believe, they can soon find themselves not believing at all.

The apostle Peter admonished the Christians of his day to "sanctify the Lord God in your hearts, and always be ready to give a defense to everyone who asks you a reason for the hope that is in you, with meekness and fear" (1 Peter 3:15). This means we must know *what* we believe and be able to explain *why* we believe it.

This workbook serves as an introduction to Christian evidences. It examines some of the evidence that supports our belief in the existence of God, the inspiration of the Bible, and the resurrection of Jesus from the dead. It will make the young Christian aware of some of the flaws in the theory of evolution. Why do we believe Jesus is the Son of God? Why should we follow the Bible today? Why does God allow suffering? What about dinosaurs? Is the earth really billions of years old? Could God have used evolution as the means of creating plant and animal life on the earth? All of these questions are addressed in this workbook.

I am grateful to Mike Hepner for taking the time to proofread this material, and to Joshua Gurtler and Carolyn Bixby for providing help with some of the material. Many of their suggestions are a part of this workbook.

Unless otherwise noted, all Bible quotations are taken from the New King James Version.

Table of Contents

Dedication

This book is dedicated to my sister, Becky Rogers.

It's not unusual for siblings to have many things in common. Among them, Becky and I both have a respect for God's word and an interest in science. Becky has earned a master's degree in forensic science with a specialty in technical investigation (the training necessary to be a crime scene investigator), while I've given my life to studying and teaching God's word. This book is a combination of both fields (the Bible and science), so it's fitting that it be dedicated to my sister.

Becky, you are my oldest best friend and one of my greatest sources of encouragement. You always have my back, and there will always be a place in my heart reserved just for you.

Evidence for the Existence of God (Part 1)

There can be no greater subject for man to consider than whether or not God exists. One's entire life hinges on the answer to this question. If God doesn't exist, there's no reason to continue with the lessons in this workbook. We're free to live by any standard we choose. However, if God does exist, we know we're accountable to Him and must strive to please Him in this life.

Since this is such an important question, we need to base our answer, and thus our faith, upon solid evidence. Is there any evidence that proves God is real? How can I know God exists?

The existence of God can't be proven by the scientific method. Science involves the study of what can be observed and repeated. God is a spirit (John 4:24) and thus can't be observed. The creation of the universe can't be repeated for our observation. Therefore, science can't prove the existence of God. However, it's important to note that science can't disprove the existence of God either. Science simply can't provide an answer for our question.

This doesn't mean there's no evidence proving the existence of God. The Bible claims God has left evidence of His existence in the created world and in the affairs of men's lives (Ps. 19:1; Rom. 1:18-20; Acts 14:15-17).

In this lesson, we're going to take a basic, common-sense approach to some of this evidence. Then, in light of this evidence, we'll ask which is the more reasonable option: to believe God exists or to believe He does not exist?

Key Passage

"For since the **creation** of the world His invisible attributes are **clearly seen**, being understood by the things that are made, even His eternal power and Godhead, so that they are **without excuse**."

- Romans 1:20

QUESTIONS

1. Why is it important for us to find an answer to the question "Does God exist?" _____

    _____

    _____

2. Can the existence of God be proven by the scientific method? Why or why not? _____

    _____

    _____

3. According to the Bible, where can we look to find evidence of God's existence?_____

    _____

    _____

The origin of the universe

Man's oldest and most basic question is one of origins: "Where did I come from?" The universe is here. Where did it come from?

To find the answer to this most basic question, we need to consider the law of cause and effect. We accept the fact that "for every effect, there must be an adequate cause that existed before the effect." We use this law daily in different situations of our life.

When it comes to the origin of the universe, there are three possible options to consider:

1. The universe has always existed.
2. The universe created itself.
3. The universe was created by something else.

1. **The universe has always existed.**
    This may seem like an easy answer to our question, but it has some problems. First,

It is an **observable fact** that the universe is **expanding**. If we were to go back far enough in time (13.8 billion years, according to the Big Bang theory), we would arrive at a time before the expansion started. All matter would be together in one location. If matter has existed forever, then it would have existed in this singular state for countless billions of years. **What could have caused it to change after it had been stable for an eternity in the past?** Scientists have no answer to this question.

it actually violates the law of cause and effect. Something had to cause the universe to exist. Second, it violates the second law of thermodynamics. This law states that everything in the physical universe is moving from an organized state to a disorganized state. In other words, the universe is actually winding down. This tells us that matter isn't eternal; thus, the universe has not always existed.

2. **The universe created itself.**

   This answer also violates the law of cause and effect. There's no scientific evidence supporting the idea that matter can spontaneously create itself. We all know that "nothing comes from nothing." This answer also violates the first law of thermodynamics, which states that neither matter nor energy can be created or destroyed. Matter can change states (for example, water can be a solid, liquid, or gas), but it'll always be the same amount of matter. Both matter and energy would be needed to bring the universe into existence, but there's no natural process that has ever created matter or energy out of nothing.

3. **The universe was created by something else.**

   Unbelievers reject this option outright, because it suggests the existence of a God they're unwilling to acknowledge. However, the first two options violate known laws of science, so unbelievers are in somewhat of a dilemma.

   The fact is, when we consider the origin of the universe, science can only take us back so far. At some point, events had to occur that violate known laws of science. Which is the more reasonable option: to conclude that there was a time when the laws of nature did not exist and matter created itself? Or to conclude that an all-powerful being created the physical universe? Both conclusions require a leap of faith at some point. Which is the more reasonable conclusion?

   When it comes to the origin of the universe, God certainly fits the criteria of the law of cause and effect. The Bible says, "For every house is built by someone, but He who built all things is God" (Heb. 3:4). The fact that the universe exists is evidence that God exists.

QUESTIONS

4. How would you explain the law of cause and effect?_____

   _____

   _____

   _____

5. Provide some reasons why the universe has not always existed. _____

    _____

    _____

    _____

6. Provide some reasons why the universe did not create itself. _____

    _____

    _____

    _____

7. In your own words, tell why all explanations for the existence of the
    universe require a leap of faith. _____

    _____

    _____

    _____

8. How does God fit the criteria for the law of cause and effect regarding
    the origin of the universe?_____

    _____

    _____

    _____

The design of the universe

As we explore the universe, we can't help but see the presence of complex order and design. When we witness such design, we naturally conclude that there was both a designer and a builder. No one argues that the great pyramids of Egypt were natural formations. We may not have witnessed their construction, but we know they were designed and built by someone.

The laptop computer on which I typed this lesson is the result of design and construction. I didn't buy a box of computer parts, shake it up, and pull out a functioning computer. No one would believe me if I tried to tell them this is how my computer was made.

The universe is much more complex than my laptop computer. The planets, comets, and asteroids in our solar system orbit the sun in such precise patterns that astronomers can predict where they'll be on any given date. We know when full moons and solar eclipses will occur. We also know that Halley's Comet will return on July 28, 2061. Our solar system runs like clockwork. No one argues that clocks exist by chance. Why then is it reasonable to conclude that the universe exists by chance?

THE EARTH

Evolutionary scientists would have us believe that life exists in abundance on many "earth-like" planets in the universe. However, just the opposite is true. Circumstances have to be just right in order for a planet to sustain life.

The earth is orbiting the right kind of star (a yellow dwarf) in the safe zone of the right kind of galaxy (a spiral galaxy). It's 93 million miles away from the sun, locked into a circular orbit. If the earth were any closer to the sun, it would burn. If it were any further away from the sun, it would freeze. The earth is tilted on its axis at 23.5°, providing us with our changing seasons.

The moon is 240,000 miles away from the earth. In addition to holding the earth at its 23.5° tilt, the moon also affects the ocean tides. If the moon were 1/5 of a mile closer to earth, the ocean tides would cover the continents with 35-50 feet of water twice a day. If it were any further away from the earth, the oceans would stagnate and life couldn't exist.

The earth's location, size, composition, structure, atmosphere, temperature, internal dynamics, as well as its many intricate cycles are evidence that it's uniquely suited to sustain life. It's not one of thousands or millions of possible inhabitable planets in the universe. It's one of a kind.

THE HUMAN BODY

We don't need to look through a telescope to find complex design in the physical universe. We can see it when we look in the mirror. The human body consists of a combination of several systems, all containing complex parts that have to work together in order for the body to function and live.

As your eyes are reading this lesson, your brain is processing the words you're reading, causing you to understand the points being made. At the same time, without you thinking about it, your neck muscles are holding your head in place so you can read. Your lungs are taking in air, allowing oxygen to replace carbon dioxide in your blood. Your digestive system is breaking down your last meal, providing nutrients and energy for your body. Your heart is pumping blood throughout your body, carrying the oxygen and nutrients to places where they're needed.

Are our bodies the product of evolution? Remember, design demands a designer, and our bodies bear the mark of a brilliant designer. As David said, "For I am fearfully and wonderfully made" (Ps. 139:14).

QUESTIONS

9. Can anyone make you believe complex mechanisms such as clocks, laptop computers, or automobiles are formed by chance? _____

10. In your own words, describe the special features that cause the Earth to be able to support life. _____

   _____

   _____

11. What are some of the complex systems found in the human body?

   _____

   _____

12. Explain how the complex order of the solar system and the human body argue in favor of a Creator._____

   _____

   _____

Conclusion

"The heavens declare the glory of God; and the firmament shows His handiwork" (Ps. 19:1).

As we consider the origin and complex design of the universe, we're left with two choices: it's either the product of chance or the product of a wise and powerful designer. The idea that the universe came about by chance is a position that violates established laws of science. There are too many variables needed in order for the earth to be able to support life. The odds of this happening by chance are mathematically impossible. The only reasonable alternative is that the universe is the result of an all-wise and powerful Creator.

We'll consider more evidence of God's existence in our next lesson.

QUESTIONS

13. Explain why it is more reasonable to believe the universe was created than to believe it has always existed or it created itself. _____

_____

_____

_____

_____

_____

_____

14. Everything in the universe exhibits complex design. Does this design argue in favor of an intelligent Designer or the product of random chance? Explain your answer. _____

_____

_____

_____

_____

_____

_____

Evidence for the Existence of God (Part 2)

In our previous lesson, we began looking at some of the evidence that proves God exists. We considered the origin of the universe and the order or design of the universe (things like the earth and the human body). Which is more reasonable: to believe these things came into existence by chance or to believe they're the creation of an all-wise and all-powerful God?

In this lesson, we'll continue to examine evidence for God's existence.

Animal Instinct and Man's Morality

Animals survive by operating upon instinct. Instinct is the innate guiding inclination in animals that allows them to do the things necessary for their survival (such as eating, migrating, reproducing, caring for their young, etc.). In many animals, these behaviors aren't learned from parents but come automatically.

For example, many different kinds of animals migrate: birds, butterflies, whales, fish, eels, etc. These animals know exactly when and where to go, even though some of them have never been there before. These animals also migrate in different ways. Some birds, such as starlings and meadow larks, fly during the day and navigate by the sun. Other birds, such as geese and European warblers, navigate by the stars at night. When the stars are obstructed, they stop flying until the sky clears and they can see the stars again.

"Even the stork in the heavens knows her appointed times; and the turtledove, the swift, and

Key Passage

"So **God created man** in His own image; in the image of God He created him; male and female He created them."

- Genesis 1:27

the swallow observe the time of their coming..." (Jer. 8:7).

Birds know how to build a nest without being taught. Newly hatched spiders know how to spin an intricate web without being taught. Newly hatched sea turtles know to head toward the water. All of these behaviors are essential for survival, but they're not learned by example. They're practiced out of instinct.

If animal instinct is the product of millions of years of evolution, how did these animals survive to evolve? Isn't it more reasonable to believe that someone "programmed" these instincts into these creatures?

When we consider mankind, we observe a drastic change in behavior. We don't operate by instinct. Sure, there are some inclinations with which we're born, but many of the survival skills practiced by instinct in animals have to be learned by humans. This indicates man has the ability to learn, think, and choose the proper way to respond to situations. Indeed, man has been created with the ability to reason (Is. 1:18).

"Come now, and let us **reason** together..."

- Isaiah 1:18

However, man does have something animals don't possess. While animals operate out of instinct, man operates with a sense of morality. Most people have a sense of right and wrong and make judgments and decisions based on these standards. We may not be in agreement with what constitutes "right" and "wrong," but we do have a sense of morality.

Where do these morals originate? Morality demands the recognition of a standard, but where did this standard originate? It didn't evolve over time, because no other creatures on earth are governed by a sense of morality. Isn't it more reasonable to accept that morality was given to man when he was created in the image of God (Gen. 1:26-27)?

QUESTIONS

1. How would you explain "animal instinct?" _____

    _____

    _____

    _____

2. Can you think of some animal instincts not mentioned in this lesson?

    _____

    _____

3. What animal instinct is mentioned in Jeremiah 8:7?_____

    _____

4. Animal behavior is guided largely by instinct. What guides man's

    behavior?_____

    _____

5. According to the Bible, how was man made differently than the animals

    (Gen. 1:26-27)? _____

    _____

    _____

Man's Universal Recognition of a Higher Power

A study of the history of man will indicate that people of all cultures have had one thing in common: they all believed in and worshiped a being greater than themselves. They may not have recognized Him as the God of the Bible, but they all acknowledged His existence. Why is this so?

The Bible says God has revealed His power and wisdom through the physical world He's created. "For since the creation of the world His invisible attributes are clearly seen, being understood by the things that are made, even His eternal power and Godhead, so that they are without excuse" (Rom. 1:20).

People of ancient cultures spent more time "observing" the natural world than many of us do today. They "saw" the fact that the evidence was pointing to—there is a God. It's no accident that many of these civilizations connected their deities with nature. It was the created world (nature) that told them there was a God.

How can we explain the universal desire of mankind to believe in and worship a higher power? Is it the product of evolution? The atheist insists that religion is a "crutch." It's seen as a weakness, not a strength. This would mean evolution produced a species that believes in something that isn't real. Isn't it more reasonable to accept that man's universal belief in a higher power argues strongly in favor of the existence of this higher power?

QUESTIONS

6. What unique thing do people from all cultures and civilizations have in common? _____

   _____

7. Looking back over history, have the majority of people been atheists or believers in a higher power?_____

   _____

8. Explain why many cultures connected their deities with nature (Rom. 1:20)? _____

   _____

   _____

The Consequences of Unbelief

Man certainly has the right to believe God does not exist. This may be a popular choice for some people, but history indicates this choice has significant consequences.

If there is no God, there's no absolute standard of right and wrong. Every person is a law unto themselves, which results in chaos, not order (Judges 21:25). Without a standard, no one really has the right to tell others that their beliefs and actions are wrong. Lines are blurred, wrong becomes right, and evil becomes good (Is. 5:20).

If there is no God, then mankind is ultimately governed by the exercise of power. It literally becomes the "law of the jungle," where the strongest rule by force and fear.

If there is no God, then we're the product of evolution, which means we're nothing more than an animal. This idea doesn't elevate man, it cheapens human life. Barbaric practices like abortion on demand and mass genocide are the results of this kind of thinking. Adolph Hitler was influenced by the writings of avowed atheist Friedrich Wilhelm Nietzsche and Charles Darwin. He took the ideas proposed by these men to their logical conclusion and murdered over six million Jews, because he saw them as undesirable and had the power to kill them.

If there is no God, then man is truly without hope. Without God, the only thing I have to live for is to pass my genes on to another generation. My life truly has no meaning. For years now, God and prayer have been removed from our schools. Is it any surprise that teen suicide is so common? When you take away God, you take away hope and purpose for life.

QUESTIONS

9. Does man have to believe God exists?_____

10. Discuss some of the consequences of choosing not to believe in God.

    _____

    _____

11. Give some examples of these consequences that you can observe in

    the world today. _____

    _____

    _____

Conclusion

The question of the existence of God has a great impact on man. There really isn't any middle ground—either God exists or He doesn't. If he does not exist, I can turn away from religion and pursue any number of things in my life on this earth. However, if God does exist, I must pursue Him and strive to know Him and His will for my life.

There's ample and valid evidence for the existence of God. What is my honest response to this evidence? Is it more reasonable to believe the universe and everything in it (including myself) is the result of chance? Or does the evidence point toward the existence of an all-wise and all-powerful God?

QUESTIONS

12. Explain how animal and human behavior argue in favor of the existence of God. _____

    _____

    _____

    _____

    _____

13. This lesson considered the consequences of not believing in God. State some of the responsibilities that accompany a belief in God._____

    _____

    _____

    _____

    _____

    _____

Creation or Evolution?

There are two explanations for the origin of man: creation and evolution. We are either created by God, or we're the product of a naturalistic process consisting of random chance.

Religion is seen as a system of faith in the unseen, while science claims to follow observable, testable, and repeatable facts. Naturalistic science finds no room for God, because He can't be observed or tested. However, it's important to remember that, while evolution is taught and accepted as a scientific fact, it hasn't been proven and is still a theory.

Some Christians believe they have to make a choice between science and the Bible. This is unfortunate and unnecessary. True science is a study of God's creation and shouldn't be surrendered because one chooses to believe in God.

In this lesson, we'll consider some things that are wrong with evolution, not from a scriptural point of view, but from a scientific point of view. Does the theory of evolution stand the test of science, or is it closer to "science fiction"?

The Theory of Evolution

The theory of evolution argues that all living organisms arose from one simple organism that originally arose from non-living matter.

Although there are variations in the theory, the basic argument is as follows:

> The earth formed and began to cool. As it did so, rain began to fall, and puddles of water were filled with the elements that make up

Key Passage

"I will praise You, for I am **fearfully** and **wonderfully** made; marvelous are Your works, and that my soul knows very well."

- Psalm 139:14

the most basic forms of living matter. Something happened (perhaps a strike of lightening) that caused these elements to join together into a chain of simple organic molecules. As these chains of molecules began to replicate, variations were produced that made the "offspring" better adapted to survive and reproduce. Over a period of 3.5 billion years, these variations have produced the vast abundance of living organisms found on this planet.

Evolutionary scientists admit there are disagreements regarding exactly how life began on this planet and exactly when and how each kingdom, phylum, class, order, family, genus, and species was developed. However, they do agree that all life came from simple organisms formed from non-living matter. Over time, genetic mutations resulted in slight changes in the offspring. These changes resulted in the variations of life we see today.

Evolutionists hold to this theory and claim it's the reasonable and logical explanation for our existence, but in doing so, they overlook some basic rules of science.

Evolution Violates the Law of Biogenesis

One of the most widely respected laws of biology is the law of biogenesis. "Biogenesis" is a compound word: *bio* means "life" and *genesis* means "beginning." Thus, this law deals with the beginning of life. This law states that life can only come from preexisting life and that living things reproduce after their own kind. This is constantly observed in the physical world and is counted on by farmers, stockmen, and breeders.

The Bible teaches the law of biogenesis. God established this law in the creation week when He commanded vegetation and animals to reproduce after their own kind (Gen. 1:11-12, 21, 24-25).

The truthfulness of this law has been demonstrated over and over. In the nineteenth century, French microbiologist Louis Pasteur disproved the popular theory of "spontaneous generation." This theory had been around for two thousand years. People believed living organisms arose from non-living matter. For instance, it was believed that lice came from dust or that maggots came from rotting flesh. Through his experiments, Pasteur proved this theory to be false, and today, "spontaneous generation" is dismissed as a myth of bygone generations.

The theory of evolution actually argues against the law of biogenesis and in favor of spontaneous generation. It claims life has arisen from non-living matter, despite the fact that science has proven this to be false.

Evolution also claims living organisms experienced genetic mutations that caused them to be more suited for survival in their environment. Through a process called "natural selection," the better suited organisms became the dominant types, and the original organisms gradually died out. The law of biogenesis says living things reproduce after their own kind. While it's true that genetic mutations do take place, science has yet to observe any "favorable" mutations. Every genetic mutation that occurs is bad, rendering the new organism defective, not better suited for survival.

Evolution Violates the Second Law of Thermodynamics

This scientific law was discussed in lesson one. It's the law of increased entropy. According to this law, as energy is transformed from one form into another, less of the total energy is available to be utilized in further transformations. In other words, left alone, all natural processes lead to a less ordered, less organized state.

There are some common examples that can help us appreciate this law. First, let's take a look at your bedroom. Left to itself, does it naturally become clean or dirty? Your room can become messy with little effort on your part, but cleaning your room requires effort. Second, have you ever played a game called "Telephone?" This game consists of a number of people sitting or standing in a line. A phrase is whispered to the first person in line, and they whisper it to the next person. This continues all the way down the line until the last person tells everyone what they've heard. The statement made by the last person is almost never the same thing that was spoken to the first person.

Evolution argues that biological systems are progressing in an upward direction—progressing from disorganized to highly complex forms of life. Science observes that systems naturally move

There's a difference between "micro-evolution" and "macro-evolution." **Micro-evolution** is when small changes take place **within a species** of animal. For instance, a breeder can crossbreed dogs and come up with a different kind of dog, but in the end, we can all tell it's a dog. **Macro-evolution** is the theory that big changes have taken place, causing organisms of **one species to change into an entirely different kind of species**. This change has not been observed by science and must be rejected. Like begets like; plants and animals reproduce after their own kind.

from order to disorder. The argument for evolution is made against this known and accepted law of science.

QUESTIONS

1. What is the law of biogenesis? _____

    _____

    _____

2. Is this "law" found in the Bible? If so, where?_____

    _____

3. Explain how the theory of evolution contradicts the law of biogenesis.

    _____

    _____

4. What is "spontaneous generation"?_____

    _____

    _____

5. What scientist disproved the idea of "spontaneous generation"?

    _____

6. Has science observed any good or favorable genetic mutations? _____

7. Explain how the theory of evolution contradicts the second law of thermodynamics._____

    _____

    _____

Evolution is a Mathematical Impossibility

What are the mathematical probabilities of evolution having taken place? What are the odds? Do they argue in favor of or against evolution?

The odds of getting a hole in one while playing golf are 1 in 5,000, while the odds of bowling a perfect game are 1 in 11,500. The odds of getting struck by lightning are one in a million. The odds of winning the Powerball lottery grand prize are 1 in 175,223,510.

Now, let's look at the odds of evolution taking place. The probability of the chance development of a very simple system composed of only 200 integrated parts is 1 out of 10^{375} (this is the number 1 with 375 zeroes after it!). Mathematicians generally consider any event with a probability of less than 1 chance in 10^{50} as having a zero possibility; in other words, they say it's impossible.

A 200-part system is considered a mathematical impossibility, yet it falls far short of any living system we know. The most basic type of protein molecule that could be classified as living is composed of at least 400 linked amino acids, each made up of a specific arrangement of four or five chemical elements, each with a unique combination of protons, neutrons, and electrons.

The chance formation of even the simplest replicating protein molecule is 1 in 10^{450}. The probability of forming the proteins and DNA for the smallest self-replicating entity is 1 in $10^{167,626}$.

So, mathematically, we all have a better chance of bowling the perfect game, getting a hole in one, winning the lottery (although we shouldn't gamble), and then being struck by lightning, than for a simple protein to be formed out of non-living matter. Is it possible that evolution has taken place? Mathematics says, "No."

No Support in the Fossil Record

Evolution is presented as a slow process. In fact, the estimated age of the earth is constantly changed to allow more and more time for evolution to have taken place. According to evolutionists, one species doesn't automatically give rise to an entirely different species. It's believed that there are "transitional links" between the species. In his groundbreaking book, *The Origin of Species*, Charles Darwin wrote, "The number of intermediate and transitional links between all living and extinct species must have been inconceivably great." He believed that, over time, the fossil record would reveal these missing links.

The fossils preserved in the earth's crust provide a kind of "written" record of events that have occurred throughout the history of this planet. If evolution took place, we should find the following things in the fossil record:

- Very simple life forms appearing
- Simple life forms gradually changing into complex life forms
- Many transitional links between different kinds of organisms

- The beginnings of new body features, not fully developed, but in the process of development

However, a study of the fossil record reveals:

- Complex life forms suddenly appearing.
- Complex life forms multiplying after their own kind.
- No transitional links between different biological families.
- No partial body features; all parts appear to be complete.

The fossil record doesn't give the evolutionist the evidence he needs. A great many fossils have been discovered since Darwin wrote his book, but none of these transitional links have been found.

QUESTIONS

8. According to mathematics, is evolution possible? _____

9. Does the fossil record support the theory of evolution? _____

10. Explain why transitional links are necessary for the theory of evolution.

    _____

    _____

11. Has the fossil record provided any evidence of transitional links? _____

Conclusion

As the great debate over the origin of the universe and mankind continues, each side must approach the issue with honesty and integrity. The Bible states how all physical matter came into existence, but the claims of the Bible mean very little to an unbeliever. In the place of creation, the unbeliever has embraced the theory of evolution as an explanation for the existence of life on this planet. However, as we've begun to show in this brief lesson, the theory of evolution doesn't stand the test of true science.

If this is the case, one wonders why smart people continue to cling to and defend bad science. The answer is simple: it's the desperate attempt of unbelievers to convince themselves that God does not exist. If He doesn't exist, then they're free to live any kind of life they choose to live.

Earlier in this lesson, we said we shouldn't gamble. The atheist is making the greatest gamble of all—he's betting his eternal soul that God doesn't exist, and the odds are not in his favor.

QUESTION

12. Let's say you are a lawyer and you have to build a case disproving the theory of evolution. State the pieces of evidence you would use to oppose evolution and explain why you would use them. _____

_____

_____

_____

_____

_____

_____

_____

_____

The Age of the Earth

I took an advanced biology class when I was in high school. This was the first time I was taught evolution as a scientific fact. The material presented in the class was persuasive, and I found myself in a dilemma faced by many other young Christians: "How do I reconcile these scientific 'facts' I'm learning with the Biblical account of creation found in Genesis chapter one?" I came up with what I believed was a great compromise: "What if God used evolution as the means of creating life on this earth? Why can't we somehow fit the millions of years of evolution into the Bible's creation week?"

I wasn't the first or only person to have such thoughts. Theistic evolution has been around for a long time. It's the result of compromising the plain teaching of the Bible with evolutionary science. In fact, I later learned that my idea already had a name: the "Day-Age Theory." This compromise offers a middle ground between creation and evolution. However, as I later came to realize, this compromise isn't only unnecessary, it's actually dangerous.

The one thing that's essential to the process of evolution is time—lots and lots of time. Today, evolutionists claim the earth is 4.5 billion years old. They've reached this conclusion, not so much because of the evidence of scientific data, but because this age provides sufficient time for evolution to have occurred. An interesting fact is that, in Charles Darwin's day, evolutionists believed the earth was only 20 million years old. As the theory of evolution becomes more complicated, the time needed increases, and thus the earth becomes "older."

Key Passage

"I have more understanding than all my teachers, for Your **testimonies** are my meditation."

- Psalm 119:99

Christians sometimes feel intimidated by the claims of evolutionary science and are quick to make unnecessary compromises. The age of the earth is one of these compromises. In this lesson, we'll consider what the Bible has to say about the age of the earth. We'll then look at some scientific facts that support the Bible's claim and then consider the danger of claiming the earth is billions of years old.

The Bible Argues for a Young Earth

While the Bible doesn't provide an exact date for the creation of the earth, it does indicate the earth is young rather than billions of years old.

BIBLE GENEALOGIES

According to the Bible, the earth is only five days older than man (Gen. 1:24-31). If we can determine how long man has been on the earth, we can calculate the age of the earth. We know it's been about 2,000 years since the time of Christ. The time span from Jesus back to Abraham is roughly 2,000 years (55 generations; Luke 3:23-34). The time span from Abraham to Adam is roughly 2,000 years (20 generations; Luke 3:34-38). This gives us a total time of 6,000 years—a young earth.

THE DAYS OF CREATION AS CONSECUTIVE 24-HOUR DAYS

The Sabbath day of rest commanded to the Children of Israel was patterned after God's creation week (Ex. 20:8-11). The Children of Israel clearly understood the creation week to be just like their own week. It didn't consist of eons of time represented as "days" but was made up of literal, consecutive, 24-hour days.

THE BEGINNING OF CREATION

In discussing the creation of man, Jesus said, "But from the beginning of the creation, God 'made them male and female'" (Mark 10:6). According to Jesus, man appeared in this world all the way back at the beginning. However, the theory of evolution claims man has appeared only recently. "Imagine that all 4.6 billion years of evolutionary time were represented by one 60-minute hour. In this illustration, animals would only have appeared in the last ten minutes, while humans would have only arrived on the scene in the last 1/100 second" (Gurtler, 29).

Consider the significance of this point. Regarding the appearance of man on this earth, we have Jesus saying one thing and man saying the exact opposite. Jesus was present at the creation of the world (Gen. 1:26; John 1:1), and He was actually involved in the creation of the world (Col. 1:16). I believe we can take His word regarding when man was created. Jesus understood the earth to be young—not billions of years old.

A LITERAL INTERPRETATION OF THE CREATION ACCOUNT IN THE NEW TESTAMENT

The New Testament gives us a clear pattern for the proper interpretation of the creation account in Genesis. If the first few chapters of Genesis were meant to be interpreted figuratively, then we could expect to see the New Testament interpret them figuratively. However, we find that the New Testament interprets these passages as accurate records of real historical events.

Jesus spoke of the creation of man, the death of Abel, and the flood of Noah's day as real events (Matt. 19:4-6, 23:35, 24:37-38). He didn't see them as myths or motifs used by Moses to explain the origin of man. Jesus had a literal interpretation of these passages of Scripture.

Paul spoke of Adam and Eve as being real people, and then he spoke of the details surrounding their creation and their fall into sin as real events (1 Cor. 11:3, 8; 2 Cor. 11:3). He used these details to explain why a woman isn't to have authority over a man in the church (1 Tim. 2:12-14). Paul's argument can't stand if it was based on something that never actually happened.

QUESTIONS

1. Explain why the children of Israel would've understood the creation week to have consisted of consecutive, 24-hour days (Ex. 20:8-11).

   _____

   _____

   _____

2. Using Mark 10:6, explain why Jesus believed in a "young" earth._____

   _____

Why does the earth appear to be so old?

How can the earth only be a few thousand years old when it looks like it's billions of years old? Think about this: how old was Adam when he was created? He was one day old. However, the Bible says he was a man, not a baby. He had the ability to think, walk, and talk. God created Adam with apparent age. He must have created the universe in the same way.

3. Think about it: what are we saying about Jesus if we insist the earth is

    billions of years old? _____

4. In your own words, explain why Paul must have believed in a literal

    interpretation of the creation account. _____

    _____

    _____

What Science Says About the Age of the Earth

One might assume all scientists believe the earth is billions of years old, but this isn't true. Some scientists believe the earth is young. What kind of evidence do they use to support this view?

POPULATION STUDIES

Experts have long been studying the earth's population and have devised formulas to calculate the number of people on the earth at any given time. These studies conclude that if man had been on the earth for only one million years, the population would be 10^{5000}. This is more people than could physically fit on the entire surface of the earth. However, using the age of 6,000 years, the studies predict a present population of five billion—much closer to the actual number of about eight billion.

EROSION

Each year, the Mississippi River deposits approximately 300 million cubic yards of sediment into the Gulf of Mexico. By studying the volume and rate of accumulation of the Mississippi River Delta, it has been determined that the delta is about 4,000 years old.

At the current observable rates, the continents would completely erode in 14 million years. According to the "Old Earth" view, the continents should've eroded a long time ago.

SHRINKAGE OF THE SUN

The sun is a huge burning ball of gas. It's eventually going to run out of fuel. In 1979, scientists were able to measure the rate of the shrinkage of the sun for the first time. They learned that the sun is shrinking at a rate of 0.1 percent every 100 years (The diameter of the sun is decreasing five feet every hour).

Using this known rate of depletion, we know that 100,000 years ago, the sun was twice as large as it is today. So, 20 million years ago, the earth would've been within the diameter of the sun. Both of these situations would've made evolution impossible, for the earth would not have been able to support life.

COSMIC DUST

The earth is constantly bombarded by particles of matter from outer space, receiving about 14 million tons each year. If the earth were 4.5 billion years old, there would be a layer of meteoritic dust about 182 feet thick. The Apollo moon landings expected to encounter a very thick layer of this dust on the surface of the moon. Instead, they found a layer only about one eighth of an inch thick. It turns out that the moon hadn't been there as long as they thought.

QUESTIONS

5. According to population studies, why is it impossible for man to have been on the earth for one million years? _____

   _____

   _____

6. Where would the earth have been in relation to the sun 20 million years ago? _____

   _____

7. Which of the scientific arguments listed above do you find to be the most convincing? Why? _____

   _____

   _____

   _____

The Consequences of Compromise

The question regarding the age of the earth is important. It forces us to consider how we're going to view the Bible and science. Specifically, are we going to allow evolutionary science to determine how we interpret the Bible, or are we going to weigh scientific claims in light of the teachings of Scripture? The choice we make will have a greater impact on us than we realize.

If we claim to believe the Bible yet insist the earth is billions of years old, we're saying evolutionary science (the religion of the unbeliever) has greater authority than the Bible. However, the Bible tells us that when man says one thing and God says another, "let God be true but every man a liar" (Rom. 3:4).

If we accept the idea that the earth is billions of years old, we must reduce the account of creation in Genesis chapter one to a myth. One can't take this passage literally and have an "old earth." This sets a very dangerous precedent. Whenever we're confronted with any proposed discrepancy from unbelievers, we're tempted to reinterpret the Scriptures as being figurative. This is already being done by many people. They say they believe in the Bible but claim that the accounts of the fall of man (Gen. 3), the global flood (Gen. 6-8), the tower of Babel (Gen. 11), and Jonah and the great fish are all myths. They doubt the accuracy of the account of the Exodus of Israel out of Egypt and the reigns of Saul and David. Then, they go on to deny the virgin birth and resurrection of Jesus Christ. You see, once we start down the road of compromise, it'll take us much further than we ever intended to go.

QUESTIONS

8. What must we do to the creation account in Genesis chapter one if we claim the earth is billions of years old? _____

    _____

9. Did Jesus and Paul believe in a literal or figurative interpretation of Genesis chapter one? _____

10. In your own words, explain the danger of choosing a figurative interpretation of Genesis chapter one. _____

    _____

Conclusion

The Bible teaches the earth is young, not billions of years old. We must avoid the temptation of viewing the Bible through evolutionary science rather than viewing science through the truth set forth in the Bible. Remember, we walk by faith, not by sight (2 Cor. 5:7). Faith comes from hearing the word of God (Rom. 10:17), not from following scientific theories.

References

Gurtler, Joshua. *Unraveling Evolution*. Bowling Green, KY: Guardian of Truth Foundation, 2006. Print.

QUESTIONS

11. Explain why it is unnecessary and dangerous to force a compromise between the teaching of the Bible and Evolutionary Science. _____

_____

_____

_____

12. Why do Evolutionists have to argue for an old earth?_____

_____

_____

_____

13. Can a Christian be a scientist? Why or why not?_____

_____

_____

_____

Dinosaurs

Dinosaurs attract the attention and interest of many people. Advertisers, entertainers, and educators know this—so we see dinosaurs everywhere. They're in movies and TV programs, advertising campaigns, sports logos, and theme parks.

Because of the natural interest generated by dinosaurs, unbelievers have used these animals as a means of promoting evolution. Most of the time when dinosaurs are mentioned on TV programs or found in museums, we're told they roamed the earth millions of years ago.

Christians have to be ready to meet this challenge. We don't have to make a choice between dinosaurs and the Bible. It's possible and reasonable to believe dinosaurs existed without accepting evolution and an old age for the earth.

The Study of Dinosaurs

The modern study of dinosaurs dates back to 1822 in England. At that time, a Dr. Gideon Mentell and his wife had a hobby of collecting fossils. While visiting a patient, she happened upon a strange looking fossilized tooth. After showing it to some friends, it was identified as the tooth of a rhinoceros. It was later shown to a friend who specialized in iguanas. He said it looked like an iguana's tooth, only much larger.

By 1842, enough of these kinds of fossils had been discovered to convince scientists that a whole group of lizard-like reptiles had once lived. The name "dinosaur" was given to these creatures (from the Greek words *deinos* and *sauros*—"terribly great lizard").

Key Passage

"Look now at the **behemoth**, which I made along with you... Can you draw out **Leviathan** with a hook, or snare his tongue with a line which you lower?"

- Job 40:15, 41:1

The word "dinosaur" didn't exist until 1842. By then, the King James Version of the Bible was already over 200 years old. The word "dinosaur" isn't in our English Bible, because the word didn't exist until after the Bible had already been translated into English.

Dinosaurs and the Bible

Just because the word "dinosaur" isn't in the Bible doesn't mean dinosaurs aren't mentioned in the Bible. We can read about these incredible creatures in different places in the Bible, including the creation account.

> "Then God said, 'Let the waters abound with an abundance of living creatures, and let birds fly above the earth across the face of the firmament of the heavens.' So God created great sea creatures and every living thing that moves, with which the waters abounded, according to their kind, and every winged bird according to its kind. And God saw that it was good" (Gen. 1:20-21).

> "Then God said, 'Let the earth bring forth the living creature according to its kind: cattle and creeping thing and beast of the earth, each according to its kind'; and it was so. And God made the beast of the earth according to its kind, cattle according to its kind, and everything that creeps on the earth according to its kind. And God saw that it was good" (Gen. 1:24-25).

Included in these statements is every kind of animal. "Great sea creatures" would include the dinosaurs that lived in the sea. "Beasts" and "everything that creeps on the earth" would include the land dinosaurs. Although now extinct, dinosaurs were a part of God's original creation.

Job 40:15-24 speaks of a creature called the "behemoth." God describes this beast as a creature that "eats grass like an ox," "moves his tail like a cedar," has "ribs like bars of iron," and who's not disturbed by a flooding of the river. Some have proposed this passage is describing a hippopotamus or an elephant, but neither of these animals has a tail like a cedar tree. We don't know the exact identity of this animal, but it certainly fits the description of the large, plant-eating dinosaurs.

Job 41 speaks of another creature called "Leviathan." This creature has a mouth full of terrible teeth and a body covered with rows of scales that can't be penetrated. He's so strong that, when he walks, the ground crashes. To him, iron is like straw and bronze is like rotting wood. Some have suggested the Leviathan was just an alligator, but people make a living wrestling alligators. God said this creature can't be captured or tamed, and that those who've tried will never do so again.

Perhaps the most remarkable feature of the Leviathan is found in verses 18-21.

> "His sneezings flash forth light, and his eyes are like the eyelids of the morning. Out of his mouth go burning lights; sparks of fire shoot out. Smoke goes out of his nostrils, as from a boiling pot and burning rushes. His breath kindles coals, and a flame goes out of his mouth."

This sounds like a description of a dragon. While we categorize a fire-breathing dragon as a mythical creature, we shouldn't be so quick to dismiss the possibility that a creature similar to a dragon once existed. Although it's on a much smaller scale, the bombardier beetle can emit an explosive blast of chemicals that's almost as hot as boiling water. Perhaps this type of defense mechanism existed on a much larger scale in a now extinct dinosaur. Also, consider the fact that many cultures have a myth concerning dragons. The fact that this "myth" is so widespread may be an indication that its origin lies more in fact than in fiction.

QUESTIONS

1. Who's credited with finding the first dinosaur fossil?_____

2. What year did the word "dinosaur" begin to be used by scientists? _____

3. Explain why the English word "dinosaur" isn't found in the Bible._____
   _____
   _____

4. Explain how dinosaurs are found in Genesis 1:20-21, 24-25. _____
   _____
   _____

5. Describe the creature called the behemoth in Job 40:15-24. _____
   _____
   _____

6. Can the creature called "Leviathan" (Job 41) be an alligator? Why or why not? _____
   _____
   _____

7. What unique feature of the Leviathan is described in Job 41:18-21? What creature does this sound like to you? _____

_____

What Happened to the Dinosaurs?

Evolutionists have offered many different theories, all of which have problems.

For example, some have suggested that, when mammals evolved and increased in number, they ate all the dinosaur eggs, thus killing off the dinosaurs. The problem with this theory is that dinosaurs aren't the only animals that laid eggs. Why didn't all the reptiles die out, along with the birds that nest on the ground?

Some have suggested that a virus killed the dinosaurs. Again, why did it only kill the dinosaurs? Other reptiles have survived to the present time.

The most popular theory suggests that the dinosaurs were made extinct because an asteroid hit the earth. The argument goes like this: "When the asteroid hit the earth, the impact threw up tons of dust, which blocked out the sun and killed mass amounts of vegetation. Without vegetation, the dinosaurs starved to death." While this theory is popular, it still has problems. Why were only dinosaurs affected? Shouldn't all animals have starved after such an impact?

Christians actually have a perfect explanation for the sudden disappearance of dinosaurs—the global flood of Genesis 6-8. Every living thing that breathed air that wasn't in the ark perished in the flood (Gen. 7:21-24). This would've included dinosaurs.

While unbelievers deny the Biblical account of the flood, the fossil record actually argues in favor of a global flood.

Consider the process by which fossils are made. Not everything that dies turns into a fossil. In fact, circumstances have to be just right in order for the remains of an animal or plant to fossilize.

1. The animal must die and be buried very quickly. Otherwise, the body will decay or be consumed by scavengers.

2. The buried remains must be in contact with circulating ground water. Over time, the minerals in the water replace the elements in the bone, and they turn into stone. This process doesn't require millions of years to take place.

3. At a later time, erosion is necessary to expose the fossil.

"Dinosaur graveyards" have been discovered in different parts of the world, including Dinosaur National Monument on the Utah/Colorado border. These graveyards contain jumbled masses of fossilized remains, suggesting great numbers of dinosaurs died suddenly and were quickly buried under a layer of sediment. This would've happened all over the earth during the flood of Noah's day.

The earth's crust is made up of different layers of rock. These layers of rock are called the "geological column." Some scientists believe these layers of rock represent different ages of the earth and assign millions of years to each layer. A fossil is dated by these scientists according to the layer of rock in which it's found. For instance, if a fossil is found in a layer of rock believed to be 160 million years old, they'll claim the fossil is that old.

The problem with this method of dating is that some fossils have been discovered lying across two of these rock layers. To which rock layer does such an animal belong, seeing as how its dead body is found in both layers? This is a problem that's not easily solved. Also, in some places in the earth's crust, these layers are inverted, with the "oldest" layers on top and the "youngest" layers on bottom. How can this be possible? Unbelievers try to come up with possibilities, but both of these problems are easily explained by the global flood of the Bible.

QUESTIONS

8. What theories have been suggested for the extinction of the dinosaurs? Identify some problems with each theory. _____

_____

_____

_____

_____

9. What event in the Bible explains the extinction of the dinosaurs?

_____

10. Describe the steps necessary in order for an animal to become a fossil.

_____

_____

_____

11. Why are "dinosaur graveyards" strong evidence for the global flood of

the Bible? _____

_____

_____

Conclusion

We know dinosaurs existed. The evidence found in the fossil record can't be denied. However, Christians aren't in the position of having to choose between believing in dinosaurs and believing the Bible. Just because the word "dinosaur" isn't found in the Bible doesn't mean they didn't exist. Did you know there are several other animals that aren't specifically mentioned in the Bible? Among them are sharks, jellyfish, kangaroos, and even cats. Why not? Consider this: the Bible was meant to be an account of God's creation, not a catalog of God's creation.

Dinosaurs aren't evidence of evolution. Dinosaurs are a part of God's creation, manifesting His wisdom and creative power.

QUESTIONS

12. How would you answer a person who said dinosaurs aren't real? _____

_____

_____

_____

_____

13. How does the Bible answer the question of whether or not dinosaurs

and man lived together at the same time?_____

_____

_____

_____

_____

Evil, Pain, and Suffering

We see it all around us. We learn of tragedies every day. Innocent people are killed in car crashes or are the victims of violent crimes. Neighborhoods are destroyed by tornados. Hospitals are full of patients fighting various diseases. People are suffering.

We can't deny the presence of evil, pain, and suffering in our world today. Unfortunately, this reality causes some people to have doubts about God. "Why did God let my loved one die? Does He care? Isn't He powerful enough to protect good people? I'm not sure if I can believe in God anymore."

The existence of evil, pain, and suffering is one of the greatest arguments set forth by unbelievers. Christians believe in an all-powerful, all-loving God, and yet the world is full of sorrow and pain. How can these two realities possibly fit together?

It's important that we have an answer to this question, not only to defend our faith before unbelievers, but to maintain our own faith as we personally experience trials and suffering in our life.

The Origin of Evil

Since God created all things, isn't it reasonable to believe God created evil?

No. The Bible doesn't say or even suggest that God created evil, pain, and suffering. Everything God created was good. As the creation week came to a close, we read "Then God saw everything that He had made, and indeed it was very good. So the evening and the morning were the sixth day" (Gen. 1:31). So, from where did evil originate?

Key Passage

"My brethren, take the prophets, who spoke in the name of the Lord, as an example of suffering and patience. Indeed we count them blessed who endure. You have heard of the perseverance of Job and seen the end intended by the Lord—that the Lord is very **compassionate** and **merciful**."

- James 5:10-11

God created man in His own image (Gen. 1:26-27). As we saw in lesson two, man wasn't created to act out of instinct like animals. Man was uniquely created with the ability to think and reason, to make choices. Out of His love for man, God gave him free will. God respects the decisions man makes, even when these decisions have painful consequences.

God didn't abandon man to exercise his free will without a warning. God has always cautioned man of the consequences of making the wrong choice. Consider the circumstances regarding the first sin.

> "And the Lord God commanded the man, saying, 'Of every tree of the garden you may freely eat; but of the tree of the knowledge of good and evil you shall not eat, for in the day that you eat of it you shall surely die'" (Gen. 2:16-17).

Notice two things. First, God gave man a choice of trees from which to eat. Second, God clearly warned man what would happen if he chose to eat from the tree of the knowledge of good and evil. Man understood the consequences of this choice (Gen. 3:1-3).

When man ate from this forbidden tree, he began to suffer the consequences of his decision.

- He felt shame for the first time (vv. 7-8).
- He felt fear for the first time (v. 10).
- Man became subject to great sorrow and pain (v. 16).
- The earth became cursed (v. 17).
- Physical death became a reality (v. 19).

This is the origin of evil, pain, and suffering in our world. It wasn't created by God. It's the consequence of man's sin.

QUESTIONS

1. Have any tragedies affected you, a loved one, or a close friend? _____

2. In your own words, explain why the existence of evil, pain, and suffering could cause people to have doubts about God._____

   _____

   _____

3. Did God create evil? Consider Genesis 1:31 in your answer. _____

   _____

4. What did God say would happen if man ate from the tree of the knowledge of good and evil (Gen. 2:16-17)?_____

   _____

   _____

5. List the consequences of this decision (Gen. 3:7-19). _____

   _____

   _____

   _____

6. Where did evil, pain, and suffering originate?_____

   _____

Why Does Man Suffer?

God gives us the freedom of choice, but He doesn't protect us from the consequences of our choices. God respects our decisions, even when our wrong choices bring consequences upon ourselves and others. Suffering isn't the result of God's impotence or indifference. Suffering is the result of man's sin. Let's consider some specific reasons why we suffer.

1. **Personal wrong choices**

   The Bible tells us we'll reap what we sow (Gal. 6:7). While we can escape the eternal consequences of our sins through Jesus Christ (Rom. 6:23), there's no promise that God will deliver us from the physical consequences of our sins. The book of Proverbs is full of warnings regarding the consequences of foolish choices. Indeed, "the way of transgressors is hard" (Prov. 13:15, KJV).

2. **Wrong choices of others**

   We can understand why we have to suffer the consequences of our own decisions, but what makes the problem of human suffering more challenging is when innocent people are called on to suffer. It just doesn't seem fair that people have to suffer because of someone else's malice or mistake.

   Remember, God has given free will to everyone, not just good people. God is no respecter of persons (Acts 10:34; Rom. 2:11). He won't grant free will to those who'll use it properly and deny it to others. While we often benefit from the good decisions made by others, we sometimes pay a price when others make bad decisions.

3. **Wrong choices of past generations**

   Decisions have a ripple effect. When you throw a rock in a pond, the force of the rock is felt strongest at the point of impact, but soon that impact is felt all across the surface of the water. The same thing is true of the decisions we make—both good and bad. Sometimes, the benefits of good decisions and the consequences of bad decisions can be "felt" for generations.

   In the ten commandments, God warned the children of Israel about the consequences of turning to idolatry. "You shall not make for yourself a carved image... you shall not bow down to them nor serve them. For I, the Lord your God, am a jealous God, visiting the iniquity of the fathers upon the children to the third and fourth generations of those who hate Me" (Ex. 20:4-5).

   When a generation of people turns their back on God, events are put into motion that will have an adverse effect on future generations. Why are innocent children starving to death in different parts of the world today? In some places, their ancestors rejected the God of the Bible and adopted beliefs in reincarnation. Such a belief has consequences. For instance, such people will not kill and eat animals for fear that they're departed loved ones. In other places, children are starving to death because their ancestors ignored Biblical principles of agriculture and have drained the ground of its nutrients (Lev. 25:1-7). What was once rich farming soil has become a sandy desert, and the people starve.

4. **Violation of God's natural law**

   Man's laws can sometimes be broken without suffering any consequences. However, we cannot break God's law without paying a price. This is true of God's spiritual laws, but it is also true of His physical laws—what we often call the laws of nature.

   For instance, if we grab something that is hot or fall from a ladder we will get hurt. Unfortunate things happen to all people, both good and bad. Time and chance happen to all of us (Eccl. 9:11-12). As we saw earlier in this lesson, the earth was cursed as a result of sin (Gen. 3:17). Because of this, the earth is subject to natural disasters—earthquakes, hurricanes, tornados, lightning strikes, floods, blizzards, etc. When these disasters occur, no person is to blame, but innocent people are sometimes injured or even killed. God will not "step in" and rescue us from such events. He has given us a great world in which to live. He is not to be blamed if it has been cursed because of sin. When we violate God's laws that govern this world, we run the risk of injury or death.

QUESTIONS

7. Has God promised to deliver us from the physical consequences of our bad decisions? _____

8. God has given us the freedom of choice. Why doesn't God keep bad people from making decisions that hurt others (Acts 10:34; Rom. 2:11)?

    _____

    _____

9. Give some reasons why innocent children are starving to death in different parts of the world._____

    _____

    _____

Benefits of Pain and Suffering

It's wrong for us to assume God would want to eliminate all pain and suffering in this world. While it's certainly undesirable from a human point of view, God is actually able to make great use of pain and suffering.

- **Pain and suffering alert us to danger.** Pain tells us something is wrong. External pain will cause us to pull our hand away from a hot object before getting badly burned. Internal pain can alert us to a severe problem, causing us to go to the doctor and receive much needed medical attention.

- **Pain and suffering are great teachers.** We learn important lessons, and they're impressed on us much more effectively if we have to suffer the consequences of wrong decisions. Sometimes, discipline is necessary in order to correct bad behavior. Corrective discipline can take many different forms, but in order for discipline to be effective, it must be unpleasant (Heb. 12:11).

- **Pain and suffering can build character.** Some of the characteristics we value and admire the most (bravery, valor, honor, courage, love, self-sacrifice, etc.) are born out of affliction (Rom. 5:3-4; James 1:2-4). There's an old Arab proverb that says, "Sunshine all the time makes a desert." We actually need some "rainy days" in our lives.

- **Pain and suffering equip us to comfort others.** "Blessed be the God and Father of our Lord Jesus Christ, the Father of mercies and

God of all comfort, who comforts us in all our tribulation, that we may be able to comfort those who are in any trouble, with the comfort with which we ourselves are comforted by God" (2 Cor. 1:3-4). You cannot tell someone, "I know how you feel," if you've never suffered like they have.

QUESTIONS

10. Describe how pain can alert us to danger._____

_____

11. What's the benefit of suffering the consequences of our bad choices?

_____

_____

12. How can enduring pain and suffering build good character? _____

_____

_____

13. How can enduring pain and suffering equip us to help others? _____

_____

_____

14. Can you think of any other benefits of pain and suffering? _____

_____

Conclusion

We can't deny the existence of evil, pain, and suffering in our world or in our own lives. While it's hard to endure and even harder to understand, the presence of evil and suffering in this world isn't a good enough reason to stop believing in God.

God has given us a beautiful world governed by natural laws. In His word, God has shown us what's right and wrong and has warned us against doing that which is wrong. God has given us freedom of choice, and He honors that choice, even when our bad decisions bring consequences on both ourselves and others. Instead of doubting God's love or denying His existence, we should use times of suffering as opportunities to grow spiritually and further strengthen our faith.

QUESTIONS

15. How did God's creation of mankind differ from His creation of the animals? _____

_____

_____

_____

16. How is God able to make use of pain and suffering? _____

_____

_____

_____

_____

_____

Is the Bible Inspired by God?

Now that we've considered ample evidence for the existence of God, we turn our attention to His word.

The Bible claims to be inspired. However, this claim by itself proves nothing. Any book can claim to be inspired by God. Is there any evidence that backs up this claim of inspiration?

The Unity of the Bible

Suppose we went to a crowded place in your community (like a mall or a busy street corner), stopped ten people at random, and asked them to tell us about God. Let's say we told them we wanted to know what God's like, what He requires of us, what makes Him happy and angry, etc. What are the chances that we'd get ten identical answers?

Now, suppose we went on to ask them about things like raising children, roles within the home and society, worship, and the afterlife. What if we asked them about their views on homosexuality, premarital sex, crime and punishment, death and suffering, etc.? Again, what are the chances that we'd get identical answers? Perhaps, by now, your experiences in life have shown you how difficult this would be.

The Bible is a collection of 66 individual books written in three different languages (Hebrew, Aramaic, and Greek), by 40 different writers from various backgrounds (including kings, soldiers, shepherds, farmers, fishermen, a doctor, a cup bearer, a tax collector, and a tent maker), on three

Key Passage

"All Scripture is given by **inspiration** of God, and is profitable for doctrine, for reproof, for correction, for instruction in righteousness, that the man of God may be complete, thoroughly equipped for every good work"

- 2 Timothy 3:16-17

- **66** books
- **3** different languages
- **40** different writers
- **3** different continents
- **1,600** years

different continents (Africa, Asia, and Europe), over a period of 1,600 years. The Bible talks about God, but it also covers hundreds of different controversial topics.

Given the scenario mentioned above, one would expect to find the Bible to be a tangled mess of confusion and contradictions. However, on investigation, we find just the opposite to be true. The message of the Bible is harmonious, manifesting perfect unity.

If ten people living in the same town at the same time can't agree on who God is and what He wants, how did these 40 different writers scattered across three continents over 1,600 years agree? The only reasonable explanation is that the writers were inspired by God.

QUESTIONS

1. Why do we need evidence that proves the Bible is inspired by God? _____

   _____

   _____

2. How many people wrote the books of the Bible?_____

3. Can you list some of their names? _____

   _____

   _____

4. How does the unity of the Bible indicate it was inspired by God?_____

   _____

   _____

The Historical and Geographical Accuracy of the Bible

Books authored by men often require corrections and updates. If the Bible were of human origin, one would expect to find numerous mistakes. However, as one reads the Bible, he finds it to be an amazingly accurate book.

There are hundreds of incidents in the Bible that can be checked against secular history and archaeology for its accuracy. The Bible is always proven to be correct.

For instance, skeptics used to make fun of the Bible's reference to the Hittites. The Hittites are mentioned over 40 times in Scripture, but there was no mention of them in any secular history or archaeological discoveries. To the skeptic, the Hittites simply didn't exist. The Bible was wrong!

> "Then, in 1906, Hugh Winckler excavated Boghazkoy, Turkey and discovered that the Hittite capital had been located in that very site. His find was all the more powerful because of the more than 10,000 clay tablets that were found in the ancient city's library and that contained the society's law system—which eventually came to be known as the Hittite Code" (Thompson, 34).

The skeptic was proven to be wrong—the Bible is right!

The book of Acts was written by Luke. It mentions 32 countries, 54 cities, 9 Mediterranean islands, and 95 people (62 of which aren't named anywhere else in the New Testament). Luke's references, where checkable, are always correct.

The Bible is too accurate to be the work of men.

QUESTIONS

5. Would you trust a book that gave you inaccurate historical data (for instance, what if your school's history book told you George Washington was the second president or that Mexico was north of the United States)? _____

Scientific Foreknowledge

The Bible is not a science book, but it does reveal scientific facts that weren't discovered by man until centuries later.

For instance, Leviticus 17:11 claims that life is in the blood. Some 3,000 years later, man discovered that blood carried life-giving oxygen and nutrients throughout the body.

"For the life of the flesh is in the blood..."

- Leviticus 17:11

Man used to believe the earth was flat. People thought Columbus was a fool for sailing west to get to India. They believed he would fall off the edge of the earth. The Bible says the earth is round (Isaiah 40:22).

Jeremiah 33:22 says the stars of heaven can't be numbered. For centuries, man believed there were about 1,000 stars. Today, scientists have suggested there are over 25 sextillion (the number 1 followed by 21 zeros) stars in the universe, and that number will likely rise as we continue to make advances in technology and can look deeper and deeper into space.

"It is He who sits above the circle of the earth..."

- Isaiah 40:22

Using Psalm 8:8 as an inspiration, Matthew Fontaine Maurry discovered and charted the ocean currents. His book *The Physical Geography of the Sea*, which first appeared in 1855, led to great improvements in shipping, and began the science of oceanography.

"As the host of heaven cannot be numbered..."

- Jeremiah 33:22

No one argues that the Bible was only written two or three hundred years ago. Even skeptics and unbelievers recognize that the Scriptures are thousands of years old. How could man have "guessed" the scientific facts that are recorded in the Bible centuries before they were discovered?

QUESTIONS

6. What claim is made about blood in Leviticus 17:11?_____

_____

7. What passage in the Bible led to the discovery of ocean currents?_____

_____

The Impartiality of the Bible

A book written by man would seek to minimize the faults of its heroes while overemphasizing their virtues. This wasn't done in the Bible. It's a perfectly impartial, historical, and amazingly objective account. Consider some of the sins of the great men of the Bible that weren't "swept under the rug."

- Noah found grace in the eyes of Lord, yet on one occasion, he became drunk with wine (Gen. 6:8, 9:20-29).

- Abraham was the friend of God, yet he lied about Sarah being his wife—twice (James 2:23; Gen. 12:10-20, 20:1-18).

- Moses served as deliverer of Israel out of Egypt and was the mediator of the covenant between God and Israel. He alone enjoyed face-to-face fellowship with God, yet wasn't allowed to enter the Promised Land, because he disobeyed God (Num. 12:7-8, 20:7-12).

- David was a man after God's own heart, yet he committed adultery and murder (Acts 13:22; 2 Sam. 11-12).

- Peter was an apostle of the Lord, yet he made numerous mistakes, including denying the Lord (Matt. 26:69-75).

The Bible is too impartial to be the work of man.

QUESTIONS

8. Identify the sins committed by the following heroes of the Bible:

    Noah _____

    Abraham _____

    Moses _____

    David _____

    Peter _____

9. Which piece of evidence discussed in this lesson do you find to be the most persuasive? Why?_____

    _____

    _____

    _____

Conclusion

This lesson has considered only a few of the pieces of evidence we need in order to know, with confidence and certainty, that the Bible is inspired by God. We'll consider another piece of evidence in our next lesson on fulfilled prophecy.

THOUGHT QUESTION

10. As in lesson three, let's say you are a lawyer and you are building a case to prove the Bible is God's inspired word. What pieces of evidence you would use to make your case? Explain why you would use them. _____

_____

_____

_____

_____

_____

_____

_____

_____

References

Thompson, Bert, *In Defense of the Bible's Inspiration*, Montgomery, AL, Apologetics Press, Inc., 2001, print

Fulfilled Prophecy

Fulfilled prophecy is perhaps the greatest piece of evidence confirming both the accuracy and divine inspiration of the Bible. Fulfilled prophecy doesn't deal with coincidence or guesswork, nor is it the product of authors who tried to trick us by "predating" their books. It's evidence of the omniscient mind of God and His sovereign power over this world.

Criteria for Valid Prophecy

Not just any kind of prediction qualifies as a prophecy of divine origin. Anyone can make vague or generic predictions and have a good chance of them coming true. For instance, predictions about the weather, election results, or who will win the Super Bowl aren't divine prophecies. In order for something to be recognized as a valid prophecy, it must meet the following conditions:

1. **True prophecy must have been delivered prior to the event.** One must be able to show that the prophecy was written prior to the fulfillment. For instance, a history book published in 2014 can't be said to "predict" the Japanese bombing of Pearl Harbor on December 7, 1941.

2. **The prophecy must be detailed and specific, not vague or general.** Anyone can say "an enemy nation" will "attack the United States" at "some date in the future." A true prophecy must contain details that are exact and unmistakable.

Key Passage

"And so we have the prophetic word **confirmed**, which you do well to heed as a light that shines in a dark place, until the day dawns and the morning star rises in your hearts."

- 2 Peter 1:19

3. **The prophecy must be beyond the power of man to foresee.** A prophecy can't be based on events in the past that make it possible to predict a repetition of these same events in the future. It's been said that history repeats itself. Things generally run in cycles. Predictions based on such observations aren't prophecies.

4. **The prophecy must have a clear, understandable, and exact fulfillment.** Moses was given the test of a true prophet. "And if you say in your heart, 'How shall we know the word which the Lord has not spoken?' When a prophet speaks in the name of the Lord, if the thing does not happen or come to pass, that is the thing which the Lord has not spoken; the prophet has spoken it presumptuously; you shall not be afraid of him" (Deut. 18:21-22). The test was simple—that which the prophet spoke in the name of the Lord had to come to pass. If it didn't, it wasn't a message from the Lord.

The Bible doesn't contain one or two prophecies. The Bible contains nearly 1,000 prophecies, each one meeting the above conditions.

QUESTIONS

1. In your own words, describe what a prophecy is. _____

    _____

    _____

2. In order for something to be a valid prophecy, it must meet at least four conditions. What are these conditions?_____

    _____

    _____

    _____

3. Why can't we dismiss Biblical prophecy as guesswork or coincidence?

    _____

    _____

4. According to Deuteronomy 18:21-22, what test determined whether or not a prophet was speaking the truth? _____

    _____

5.   How many prophecies are found in the Bible?

_____

There are a number of different kinds of prophecies in the Bible. In this lesson, we'll examine some Messianic prophecies and prophecies regarding groups of people (cities or nations), along with individuals.

The Destruction of Tyre

Tyre was a major seaport on the Phoenician coast. It actually consisted of two cities: a settlement on the mainland and a small island city about a half mile off shore. Its strategic location made the city virtually impregnable.

In 586 BC, Ezekiel delivered a prophecy against this city. Ezekiel 26:1-14 actually records seven specific prophecies against Tyre:

- Many nations would come up against the city (v. 3).

- The walls and towers of the city would be broken down (v. 4).

- Even the dust of the city would be scraped away, leaving the city as a bare rock (v. 4).

- It would become a place for the spreading of nets (vv. 5, 14).

- The first nation to come against Tyre would be Babylon, led by Nebuchadnezzar (v. 7).

- The city's stones, timber, and soil would be thrown into the sea (v. 12).

- The city would never be rebuilt (v. 14).

Within a few years of Ezekiel's prophecy, Nebuchadnezzar besieged the mainland city (v. 7). Most of its citizens fled to the island. After a 13-year siege, the mainland city was deserted. The city was not yet destroyed, but its influence was severely weakened.

"I will make you like the top of a rock; you shall be a place for spreading nets, and **you shall never be rebuilt**, for I the Lord have spoken,' says the Lord God."

- Ezekiel 26:14

In 332 BC, Alexander the Great mounted a seven-month siege upon the island city. His army reached the city by building a 200-foot wide causeway from the mainland to the island. The causeway was built by scraping the debris and dirt from the city's ruins on the mainland into the sea (v. 12).

Tyre was rebuilt during the time of the Roman Empire and achieved a degree of prosperity. Jesus even passed through that region and interacted with people there (Matt. 15:21-28; Mark 7:24-31). However, in AD 1291, the island city was completely destroyed and has remained in ruins ever since. What was once an important city was made a place where fishermen spread their nets (vv. 5, 14).

Every one of the prophecies made by Ezekiel have come true.

QUESTIONS

6. Describe some of the details concerning Ezekiel's prophecy against Tyre._____

_____

_____

_____

7. What use did Alexander the Great make of the stones, timber, and soil of Tyre (Ezek. 26:12)?

_____

_____

Prophecies Regarding Individuals

King Josiah. In 1 Kings 13:1-2, a prophecy was made against the altar erected by Jeroboam that specifically mentioned a child king named Josiah and born to the house of David, sacrificing the priests, and burning men's bones upon the altar. Josiah fulfilled this prophecy 300 years later (2 Kings 23:15-16).

"...Thus says the Lord: 'Behold, a child, **Josiah** by name, shall be born to the house of David..."

- 1 Kings 13:2

"Thus says the Lord to His anointed, To **Cyrus**, whose right hand I have held..."

- Isaiah 45:1

King Cyrus. Isaiah 44:28-45:1 speaks of a man who would see to it that Jerusalem and the temple would be rebuilt. His name was mentioned: Cyrus. One hundred fifty years later, Cyrus came to the throne and saw to it that the Jews were allowed to return from captivity and rebuild the temple (Ezra 1:1-4).

To help us appreciate the significance of this prophecy coming true, this would be the equivalent of finding a book published in 1858 naming Barack Obama as the first African American to be elected as President of the United States. Prophecies this exact are beyond the realm of coincidence or guesswork.

Messianic Prophecies

There are 332 prophecies in the Old Testament that are fulfilled in the life of Jesus Christ. These are called Messianic Prophecies, because they refer to the life and work of the Messiah. These prophecies refer to many different and specific details regarding the Messiah.

HIS LINEAGE

- Born of a woman (Gen. 3:15; Gal. 4:4)
- Born of the seed of Abraham (Gen. 22:18; Luke 3:34)
- Born of the tribe of Judah (Gen. 49:10; Heb. 7:14)
- Born of the royal lineage of David (2 Sam. 7:12; Luke 1:32)
- Born of a virgin (Is. 7:14; Matt. 1:22-23)

TIME AND PLACE OF HIS BIRTH

- During the Roman Empire (Dan. 2:44; Luke 2:1)
- At Bethlehem (Micah 5:2; Luke 2:4-7)

HIS NATURE

- He would be human and divine; eternal (Micah 5:2; John 1:1, 14)
- He would be gentle and compassionate (Is. 42:1-4; Matt. 12:15-21).
- He would be submissive to God (Ps. 40:7-8; Heb. 10:5-10; Phil. 2:5-8).

HIS DEATH

- He would be betrayed by a friend (Ps. 41:9; John 13:18).
- He would be betrayed for thirty pieces of silver (Zech. 11:12; Matt. 26:15).
- He would be silent before His accusers (Is. 53:7; Matt. 26:63, 27:12-14).
- His hands and feet would be pierced (Ps. 22:16; John 20:24-27).

- He would die with the wicked (Is. 53:9; Matt. 27:38).
- But He would be buried with the rich (Is. 53:9; Matt. 27:57-60).

We'll consider the subject of Messianic prophecies again in lesson eleven.

QUESTIONS

8. What child king was mentioned by name 300 years before he was born (1 Kings 13:1-2)? _____

9. What important work did king Cyrus accomplish (Is. 44:28)? _____

   _____

10. How many prophecies are there about Jesus in the Old Testament?_____

Fulfilled Prophecy Gives Us Confirmation

Prophecies were made for the purpose of proving the power of God and the validity of His Word.

- **The omniscience and sovereignty of God:** God challenged the idols to tell of things to come (Is. 41:22-23). He said if they were able to do so, it would have proven they were really gods. Of course, they couldn't speak, for they were made of wood and stone. However, God was able to pass this test (Is. 46:8-11).

- **The deity of Jesus Christ:** Jesus based His identity as the Son of God on the prediction that He would rise from the dead in three days (John 2:19-22). He fulfilled this prophecy, thus proving He is the Son of God.

- **The inspiration of the Bible:** Peter claimed the prophetic word of the Old Testament was

"Show the things that are to come **hereafter**, that we may know that you are **gods**..."

- Isaiah 41:23

confirmed and established as being true (2 Peter 1:19-21). Fulfilled prophecy proves the Bible's claim for divine inspiration (2 Tim. 3:16-17). It also tells us we must believe the things written in the New Testament, for they'll come true just as surely as the predictions recorded in the Old Testament have come true.

QUESTIONS

11. In your own words, describe the challenge God set forth in Isaiah 41:22-23. How could these idols prove they were gods?_____

_____

_____

_____

12. Did God pass this challenge (Is. 46:8-11)?_____

13. What prophecy did Jesus make concerning Himself (John 2:19-22)?

_____

_____

14. Describe how fulfilled prophecy is evidence that the Bible is inspired by God._____

_____

_____

QUESTIONS

15. In your own words, explain how fulfilled prophecy is evidence that the Bible is inspired by God._____

_____

_____

_____

_____

_____

16. What details of Jesus' life are described in the prophecies of the Old

   Testament?_____

   _____

   _____

   _____

   _____

   _____

   _____

Conclusion

The Bible has been criticized and challenged by men for many years. However, the honest skeptic must deal honestly with the evidence.

Prophecy can't be passed off as coincidence or guesswork. The details given in the prophecies recorded in the Bible are too specific and too numerous to be ignored. Fulfilled prophecy lifts the Bible above and beyond the possibility of human authorship. Indeed, all Scripture is given by the inspiration of God.

The Sufficiency and Relevancy of the Bible

We're living in an age in which there are more copies of the Bible available than ever. The Bible can be purchased in any number of stores or accessed for free online. However, this increase in availability doesn't seem to have produced an increase in demand. There just doesn't seem to be very many people interested in learning what the Bible has to say.

People still need answers to religious, philosophical, and moral questions. However, many people are turning to talk shows, self-help books, and internet blogs to find the answers to these important questions. To some, the Bible seems insufficient. To others, the Bible is out of date.

Does the Bible still provide the answers we need? Is it still a lamp to our feet and a light to our path (Ps. 119:105)? Is the Bible up to the task, or do we need something in addition to the Bible to help us understand the will of God or get the most out of this life? We'll address these important questions in this lesson as we discuss the all-sufficiency and relevancy of the Bible.

The All-Sufficiency of the Bible

When we're talking about the sufficiency of the Bible, we're addressing the question of whether or not the Bible is enough. Is the Bible all we need, or do we need something in addition to the Bible in order to fully understand the will of God?

The Bible actually addresses the question of its sufficiency. Consider the following passages of Scripture.

Key Passage

"All Scripture is given by inspiration of God, and is profitable for doctrine, for reproof, for correction, for instruction in righteousness, that the man of God may be **complete**, **thoroughly equipped** for every good work."

- 2 Timothy 3:16-17

"All Scripture is given by inspiration of God, and is profitable for doctrine, for reproof, for correction, for instruction in righteousness, that the man of God may be complete, thoroughly equipped for every good work" (2 Tim. 3:16-17). What else do we need if the Bible makes us complete and thoroughly equipped for every good work?

"And truly Jesus did many other signs in the presence of His disciples, which are not written in this book; but these are written that you may believe that Jesus is the Christ, the Son of God, and that believing you may have life in His name" (John 20:30-31). Notice, the Bible never claims to be a record of everything Jesus ever said or did. However, it does contain everything we need in order to believe in Jesus and have eternal life.

"Do not **add to** His words, lest He rebuke you, and you be found a **liar**."

- Proverbs 30:6

"For I testify to everyone who hears the words of the prophecy of this book: If anyone adds to these things, God will add to him the plagues that are written in this book; and if anyone takes away from the words of the book of this prophecy, God shall take away his part from the Book of Life, from the holy city, and from the things which are written in this book" (Rev. 22:18-19, c.f. Deut. 4:2; Prov. 30:5-6). God warns man not to add to or take away from His Word.

"For as the rain comes down, and the snow from heaven, and do not return there, but water the earth, and make it bring forth and bud, that it may give seed to the sower and bread to the eater, so shall My word be that goes forth from My mouth; it shall not return to Me void, but it shall accomplish what I please, and it shall prosper in the thing for which I sent it" (Isa. 55:10-11). God's Word is up to the task. It'll accomplish what God intended for it to accomplish.

We can have confidence in the all-sufficiency of the Bible.

QUESTIONS

1. What do we mean when we speak of the all-sufficiency of the Bible?

    _____

    _____

2. How does 2 Timothy 3:16-17 address the question of whether or not
    the Bible is sufficient for man's needs? _____

    _____

    _____

3. The Gospel of John didn't record every word Jesus spoke or every
    miracle He performed (John 20:30-31). In fact, there are some
    questions the Bible simply doesn't address (Deut. 29:29). How then can
    the Bible claim to be sufficient? _____

    _____

    _____

4. What does God say about His Word in Isaiah 55:11? _____

    _____

    _____

The Relevancy of the Bible

The word *relevant* means "bearing upon or relating to the matter in hand;
pertinent, to the point." When we ask if the Bible is relevant, we're asking
whether or not the Bible has any bearing on our lives today. Does the Bible
relate to my life? Is it an appropriate book for me to reference? Does it
satisfy my needs, or do I need to toss it aside and look elsewhere for help
and guidance in my life?

Let's consider some simple facts to help us answer this important question.

GOD AND HIS WORD HAVE NOT CHANGED

A lot of time has passed since the Bible was written, but that doesn't mean
God has changed. How do we know this to be true? A lot of time passed
while the Bible was being written (1,600 years), yet God is the same at

the end of the Bible as He was at the beginning of the Bible. God doesn't change (Mal. 3:6; Heb. 13:8).

Time doesn't have any effect on God. He doesn't grow any wiser or more tolerant with the passing of time. God has the same attitude toward sin and evil today as He had in the beginning.

This means God's word hasn't changed. "Forever, O Lord, Your word is settled in heaven" (Ps. 119:89). Notice, God's word is settled (i.e., established, unalterable, set in stone, etc.) forever (i.e., there will never be a time in which God's word will change). The things God condemned in His word over 2,000 years ago are still condemned today.

QUESTIONS

5. What does Malachi 3:6 say about God?_____

    _____

6. How would you explain the significance of God's word being settled

    forever (Ps. 119:89)? _____

    _____

7. Explain why changes in society (for example, the acceptance of same-

    sex marriage) don't change what God's word says about such subjects.

    _____

    _____

THE NEEDS OF MANKIND HAVE NOT CHANGED

The philosophical needs of mankind have never changed. We still need answers to the most basic of questions: "Where did I come from? Why am I here? Where am I going?" Man has been searching for the answers to these questions throughout history.

In his sermon to the people of Athens, the apostle Paul answered all three of these questions. Where did we come from? We came from God (Acts 17:24-26). Why are we here? To seek God (vv. 27-28). Where are we going? To meet God in judgment (vv. 30-31).

Man also has spiritual needs. Many people have serious problems dealing with guilt, despair, depression, doubt, hopelessness, and fear. While men struggle to understand what causes these kinds of problems, the Bible

. All of the problems we face
...at we learned in the lesson on
also provides the only real solution to
...ugh obedience to the gospel of Jesus Christ

...CIETY HAVE NOT CHANGED

P...   ...to look at recent advancements and observe how things have
cha... ...d. Yes, societies do go through changes, but some things never
really change. Some people may be surprised to learn that the Bible
addresses and offers solutions to problems we're facing as a society today.

- Crime and punishment (Eccl. 8:11)
- Theft (Eph. 4:28)
- The role of civil government (Rom. 13:1-6)
- Prejudice (Acts 10:34-35; Matt. 7:12)
- Welfare abuse (2 Thess. 3:10)
- Unwed pregnancies (1 Cor. 6:18; Heb. 13:4)
- Same-sex marriage (Matt. 19:4-6)
- Family problems (Col. 3:18-21)

These problems are real. The Bible addresses all of them and many more.

QUESTIONS

8. Explain how the Bible addresses our philosophical needs. _____

_____

9. Explain how the Bible addresses our spiritual needs._____

_____

10. Can you think of some social needs addressed in the Bible that weren't
    covered in this lesson? _____

_____

_____

11. Do you believe the Bible is relevant to your life today?_____

Conclusion

The all-sufficiency and relevancy of the Bible need to be considered in a study of evidences. It really doesn't matter if we believe the Bible is inspired by God if we fail to appreciate the fact that it has direct application to our life today.

The Bible has stood the test of time and honest criticism. It's not a collection of ancient myths or an outdated relic. It's the living and eternal word of God. It stands alone as a unique source of knowledge, providing real answers to our most important questions. It gives us the standards and guidance we need, both as individuals and as a society. Most importantly, it's the only book that tells us how to receive eternal life.

QUESTIONS

12. If the Bible is sufficient, explain what use we have for other books (even workbooks like this one) that help us understand the Bible. _____

_____

_____

_____

_____

_____

13. Explain why the Bible is relevant to your life today. _____

_____

_____

_____

Why I Believe Jesus Is the Son of God (Part 1)

One day, Jesus asked His disciples what people were saying about Him. They answered, "Some say John the Baptist, some Elijah, and others Jeremiah or one of the prophets" (Matt. 16:14). People were saying all kinds of things about Jesus when He walked this earth. Some people believed He was a good man; others believed He was a deceiver and a troublemaker (John 7:12, 9:16).

Jesus followed their response with an even more important question: "But who do you say that I am?" (v. 15). With this question, Jesus made His identity a personal matter with His disciples. It mattered little what others were saying about Him. The thing that mattered was what they believed.

The same thing is true for us today. Everyone around us seems to have an opinion about Jesus Christ. Some deny His existence and claim He's a myth. Some believe He was just a man, while others believe He was a prophet of God. Christians claim Him as their Lord and Savior. However, what matters is what you believe about Jesus—who do you say that He is?

The religion of Jesus Christ is a system of faith, but it's not a leap of faith. One's acceptance of Jesus as the Son of God shouldn't be based on one's opinion, family traditions, or social beliefs. This belief should be based on evidence. In this lesson and the one to follow, we'll consider some of the evidence that proves Jesus is the Son of God.

Key Passage

"Men of Israel, hear these words: Jesus of Nazareth, a Man attested by God to you by **miracles**, **wonders**, and **signs** which God did through Him **in your midst**, as you yourselves also know."

- Acts 2:22

QUESTIONS

1. Does everyone believe Jesus is the Son of God? _____

2. Explain why it's important that we believe Jesus is the Son of God (consider John 8:24; 20:30-31 in giving your answer). _____

_____

3. In this lesson, we're examining the evidence that proves Jesus really is the Son of God. Do you think a search for such evidence indicates a lack of faith on our part? Why or why not? _____

_____

The Way Jesus Spoke

Jesus did much teaching when He walked this earth. However, the Bible makes it clear that Jesus didn't teach or speak like the scribes and rabbis of His day.

On one occasion, some officers were sent to arrest Jesus (John 7:32). He was teaching when they found Him. The officers returned empty-handed. When they were asked why they didn't arrest Jesus, they responded, "No man ever spoke like this Man!" (v. 46). Jesus didn't "talk His way out of a ticket" like some people try to do today. These officers were so impressed with His teaching that they dared not lay a hand on Him. They realized there was something different about Him.

The Gospel of Matthew tells us that what made Jesus different from other teachers of His day was that He spoke with authority. "And so it was, when Jesus had ended these sayings, that the people were astonished at His teaching, for He taught them as one having authority, and not as the scribes" (Matt. 7:28-29). The scribes and rabbis quoted Scripture to authorize their message and, for that, they demanded respect from the Jews. Jesus talked as if His words were Scripture. He talked the way God would talk. The people recognized this and determined He was different from other men.

Jesus was also a master debater. His enemies often tried to test Him or trap Him in His words before the multitudes (Matt. 21:23-27, 22:15-46). They were trying to expose Him as a fraud and turn the people against Him. Every time Jesus was tested, He answered in a way that exposed His enemies and caused the people to marvel at His words. His enemies hated His words, but "the common people heard Him gladly" (Mark 12:37).

QUESTIONS

4. Describe how the people responded to the Lord's teaching in John 7:40-44.

_____

5. Why didn't the officers arrest Jesus (John 7:46)?

    _____

    _____

6. What made the teachings of Jesus different
    from those of the scribes and rabbis of His day
    (Matt. 7:28-29)? _____

    _____

    _____

7. What happened to those who tried to trap
    Jesus in His words (Matt. 22:22, 33, 46)? _____

    _____

    _____

The Claims Jesus Made

Some of the most significant things Jesus said
were the claims He made about Himself. Consider
the following:

- He claimed to be the Messiah (John 4:25-26).
- He claimed to have come down from heaven
  (John 6:38).
- He claimed to be the "I AM" (John 8:58).
- He claimed to be equal with God (John 10:30).
- He claimed to be the only means of obtaining
  eternal life (John 14:6).
- He acknowledged that He was the Christ and
  the Son of God (Matt. 26:63-64).
- He claimed the ability to forgive sins (Mark 2:5).

These claims weren't mistaken by the enemies of
the Lord. In fact, on some occasions, they sought
to kill Him because He was claiming to be deity
(John 5:17-18, 8:59, 10:31). They clearly understood
what Jesus was saying about Himself (John 10:33);
they simply didn't believe Him.

"The Jews
answered
Him, saying...
'You, being a
Man, **make
Yourself
God**.'"

- John 10:33

Jesus never retracted these statements, not even under the threat of death. In fact, it was the admission of His belief that He was the Son of God that caused the Sanhedrin to deliver Him over to Pilate to be put to death (Matt. 26:65-66).

QUESTIONS

8.   What do you think is the most impressive claim Jesus made about Himself? _____

_____

9.   Did the Jews understand the claims Jesus made about Himself (John 10:33)? _____

10. What was Jesus saying about Himself when He said He was "I AM" (John 8:58; Ex. 3:13-14)?

_____

The Miracles That Backed up His Claims

Anyone can claim to be the Son of God. Many people have claimed to be the Messiah, and there's no doubt many more will. However, Jesus was the first and only person who backed up these claims by performing miracles.

In Mark 2:5, Jesus claimed to possess the ability to forgive sins. Some scribes heard Jesus make this claim and began to reason within their hearts, "Why does this Man speak blasphemies like this? Who can forgive sins but God alone?" (v. 7). They were correct in their understanding that a claim to forgive sins was essentially a claim to be God. Jesus went on to perform a miracle to back up His claim. He exercised divine power and healed the paralytic, thus proving He possessed the divine power to forgive sins (vv. 8-12).

The miracles performed by Jesus were a testament to His identity as the Messiah (Acts 2:22). Some

"Then the chief priests and the Pharisees gathered a council and said, "What shall we do? For this Man works **many signs**."

- John 11:47

of the Jews were honest enough to acknowledge this truth (John 3:2). His enemies, however, weren't honest regarding His miracles. They couldn't deny that Jesus performed miracles (John 11:47), but they tried to cover them up (John 12:9-11) and claimed Jesus performed miracles by the power of Satan (Matt. 9:34, 12:24).

The New Testament records about 35 miracles that Jesus performed. Not every miracle performed by Jesus was recorded (John 21:25), but the ones that were recorded have been preserved so we can believe Jesus is the Son of God and thus have life through His name (John 20:30-31).

QUESTIONS

11. What did Jesus do to back up His incredible claims? _____

    _____

12. Did Jesus' enemies deny that He performed miracles? _____

13. Explain why some of the Jews claimed Jesus cast out demons by the power of Beelzebub, the ruler of demons (Matt. 9:34, 12:24). _____

    _____

    _____

14. Why were the miracles of Jesus recorded (John 20:30-31)? _____

    _____

Conclusion

As was the case in the First Century, many people today believe many different things regarding Jesus of Nazareth. While people can have their own ideas and opinions, the thing that really matters is what we believe regarding Jesus—who do we say that He is, and why do we say it?

In our next lesson, we'll continue to look at the evidence that supports Jesus' claim to be the Christ, the Son of God.

QUESTIONS

15. What did some people believe about Jesus while He was living? _____

    _____

    _____

16. Some people believe Jesus was a good man who taught the truth, but He was not the Son of God. Jesus made several claims that He was the Son of God. In light of these claims, is it possible for Jesus to be "just a good man"? Why or why not? _____

_____

_____

_____

_____

17. Why is it important that we believe Jesus is the Son of God? _____

_____

_____

_____

Why I Believe Jesus Is the Son of God (Part 2)

In this lesson, we'll continue our study of the evidence that backs up the claim that Jesus is the Christ, the Son of God.

What Others Said About Jesus

Jurors in a trial are asked to reach a verdict based on different kinds of evidence. One very reliable form of evidence is what we call "eyewitness testimony." This is when a person who saw the events in a case is called on to tell the jurors what they saw.

The New Testament is a document recording the testimony of eyewitnesses. None of us has ever seen or heard Jesus, but many of the people recorded in the New Testament did see Him. How did those who came into contact with Jesus react to His claims and His miracles?

- His mother believed in Jesus' power to work miracles (John 2:3-5).

- Peter confessed Jesus was the Christ, the Son of the living God (Matt. 16:16).

- John said he had seen, heard, and touched the Son of God (1 John 1:1-4).

- Thomas doubted Jesus had risen from the dead. He said he wouldn't believe unless he saw the evidence for himself. When Jesus appeared to him, Thomas responded by saying, "My Lord and my God!" (John 20:24-29).

- Paul was the most fierce persecutor of Christianity (Acts 22:4-5, 26:9-11; Gal. 1:13), but he converted and gave his life to preaching the

Key Passage

"And truly Jesus did **many other signs** in the presence of His disciples, which are not written in this book; but these are written that **you may believe** that Jesus is the Christ, the Son of God, and that believing you may have life in His name."

- John 20:30-31

faith he'd once tried to destroy (Gal. 1:23). The only thing that explains his conversion is that he came to believe that Jesus is the Son of God.

- After witnessing the events at Calvary, the centurion overseeing the Lord's crucifixion concluded, "Truly this was the Son of God!" (Matt. 27:54).

We weren't alive when Jesus was on the earth, but these people were. Some of them were the Lord's friends and followers, one was His enemy, and one didn't care who He was (the centurion)—but they all agreed He was the Son of God.

QUESTIONS

1. In your own words, describe what "eyewitness testimony" is and why it's so important. _____

    _____

    _____

2. What did those who were closest to Jesus believe about Him? _____

    _____

3. How can you explain Paul's conversion? _____

    _____

    _____

4. What makes the centurion's testimony so important? Did he have an agenda when he claimed that Jesus was the Son of God? _____

    _____

    _____

Fulfilled Prophecy

We've already discussed the importance of fulfilled prophecy earlier in this book. Fulfilled prophecy is the greatest argument for both the inspiration of the Bible and for identifying Jesus as the Son of God.

Jesus made some very detailed predictions. For instance, He spoke about the nature of His death and His resurrection (Matt. 20:17-19; John 2:19). He predicted that Peter would deny Him three times before a rooster crowed twice (Mark 14:30). He also spoke of the destruction of Jerusalem (Matt. 24:1-35), an event that occurred in 70 AD.

If these events hadn't come to pass, Jesus would've been exposed as a false prophet and been subject to death under the Law of Moses (Deut. 18:20-22). However, these events did come to pass, further proving that Jesus was who He claimed to be.

Jesus was also the subject of Old Testament prophecy. There are 332 prophecies in the Old Testament that were fulfilled in the life of Jesus. Here are just a few of these prophecies:

- His birthplace—Bethlehem (Micah 5:2; Matt. 2:1)

- He'd be born of a virgin (Is. 7:14; Matt. 1:20-23)

- He'd have a forerunner (Is. 40:3; Mal. 3:1; Matt. 3:1-3, 17:10-13)

- He'd ride on a donkey (Zech. 9:9; Matt. 21:1-11)

- He'd be betrayed for 30 pieces of silver (Zech. 11:12-13; Matt. 26:14-16)

- He'd be killed with transgressors (Is. 53:12; Matt. 27:38)

- He'd be buried in a rich man's tomb (Is. 53:9; Matt. 27:57-60)

- His hands and feet would be pierced (Ps. 22:16; John 20:25-27)

- Men would cast lots for His clothes (Ps. 22:18; Matt. 27:35)

- He'd rise from the dead (Ps. 16:10; Acts 2:31).

What is the likelihood that one person could've fulfilled all 332 of these prophecies?

> "The following probabilities are taken from Peter Stoner in *Science Speaks* to show that coincidence is ruled out by the science of probability. Stoner says that by using the modern science of probability in reference to eight prophecies... 'We find that the chance that any man might have lived down to the present time and fulfilled all eight prophecies is 1 in 10^{17}.' That would be 1 in 100,000,000,000,000,000, in order to help us comprehend this staggering probability, Stoner illustrates it by supposing that 'we take 10^{17} silver dollars and lay them on the face of Texas. They will cover all of the state two feet deep. Now, mark one of these silver dollars and stir the whole mass thoroughly, all over the state. Blindfold a man and tell him that he can travel as far as he wishes, but he must pick up one silver dollar and say that this is the right one. What chance would he have of getting the right one? Just the same chance that the prophets would have had of writing these eight

prophecies and having them all come true in any one man...'" (*Evidence That Demands A Verdict* 167).

After Jesus fulfilled these eight prophecies, He had 324 to go! Fulfilled prophecy is one of the greatest pieces of evidence that proves Jesus is the Son of God.

QUESTIONS

5. Jesus was a prophet. What are some of the prophecies Jesus made (Matt. 20:17-19; Mark 14:30; Matt. 24:1-35)? _____

   _____

   _____

   _____

6. In light of Deuteronomy 18:20-22, explain why it was important for every prophecy made by Jesus to come true. _____

   _____

7. How many prophecies were made about the Messiah in the Old Testament?_____

8. What is the mathematical probability that Jesus could've fulfilled just eight of these prophecies? _____

Does Jesus Fit the Profile of the Son of God

When a crime is committed, a sketch artist will sometimes talk to a witness and come up with a drawing of what the perpetrator looks like. This picture assists police officers in apprehending the suspect. They look for people who have the same features and characteristics that were described by the witness.

In the Old Testament, we have a fairly good "picture" of what God is like. We learn of His character and attributes. If Jesus claimed to be the Son of God, we should expect Him to have these same characteristics and attributes. As we read the New Testament, we learn that Jesus is:

- Omniscient (John 16:30).
- Omnipresent (Matt. 18:20, 28:20).
- Omnipotent (Matt. 28:18).

- Holy (1 Pet. 2:22).
- Sovereign (Col. 1:15-17).
- Eternal (John 1:1).
- Immutable (Heb. 13:8).
- Forgiving (Mark 2:5-7).

(Feel free to look up some of these words if you don't know the meaning of them.)

Jesus also taught that only God was to be worshiped (Matt. 4:10). However, He allowed men to worship Him and accepted their worship (Matt. 8:2, 14:33; John 9:38). Peter refused to allow Cornelius to worship him (Acts 10:25-26), and the angel refused to allow John to worship him (Rev. 19:10, 22:8-9).

Jesus was everything on earth in the flesh that God is (Col. 2:9). He certainly fits the profile of the Son of God. He's the "Man" we're looking for!

QUESTIONS

9. Name and discuss some of the characteristics and attributes of deity, and explain how Jesus possesses these same attributes. _____

_____

_____

_____

10. Why would Jesus allow men to worship Him? Consider Matthew 4:10 in your answer. _____

_____

_____

11. What happened to Herod when he allowed men to worship him as a god (Acts 12:20-23)? _____

_____

Conclusion

Jesus claimed to be the Son of God. What are we going to do with this claim?

In his book *Evidence That Demands a Verdict*, Josh McDowell sets forth the three alternatives available to man in determining who Jesus really is. If we believe the claim that Jesus is the Son of God, we must accept the fact that Jesus is God. If we reject this claim as being false, we have two alternatives regarding Jesus: He either knew these claims weren't true and thus was a liar, or He didn't know these claims were untrue and was Himself deceived. In short, Jesus is either the Lord, a liar, or a lunatic.

Jesus asked Peter, "Who do you say that I am?" (Matt. 16:15). This is the question every one of us must answer. What do you believe about Jesus? Who do you say He is? The answer to this question will determine your eternal destiny (John 20:30-31).

QUESTION

12. As in lessons three and seven, let's say you are a lawyer and you are building a case to prove that Jesus is the Son of God. What pieces of evidence would you use to make your case? Explain why you would use them. _____

_____

_____

_____

_____

_____

_____

References

McDowell, Josh. *Evidence That Demands a Verdict, Volume One*, San Bernardino, CA, Here's Life Publishers, 1992, print

Lesson 12

Why I Believe Jesus Rose from the Dead (Part 1)

The resurrection of Jesus Christ from the dead is the very basis for the truth of Christianity. This one event validates everything Jesus claimed, taught, and accomplished while He was on the earth (Rom. 1:4). As such, the resurrection of Christ and Christianity either stand or fall together.

Jesus Himself based His identity as the Son of God upon His resurrection. Twice, when asked for a sign, He gave His future resurrection as evidence that He was who He claimed to be (John 2:19-22; Matt. 12:38-40). If Jesus had failed to come forth from the grave the third day after His death, He would've been proven to be a fraud. He would've either been a liar for saying things He knew weren't true, or He would've been a lunatic for believing things about Himself that were not true. However, if His tomb was found empty, then He was who He claimed to be: the Son of God.

> "The resurrection is the foundation upon which we base our faith and hope in Christ. Even the enemies of Christ know this. If the resurrection can be disproven, then the entire Bible is nullified as a claimant for valid faith. But if it is true, then it stands as the single greatest testimony to the validity of the Scriptures and the Christian faith. So the question before us now is, did Jesus really rise from the dead?" (Moyer, 37)

Christianity is a system of faith. We accept it by faith. However, it's not a leap of faith. Everything we believe is based on good, solid evidence, including the resurrection of Jesus Christ from the

Key Passage

"For I delivered to you first of all that which I also received: that Christ died for our sins according to the Scriptures, and that He was buried, and that He **rose again** the third day according to the Scriptures."

- 1 Corinthians 15:3-4

dead. What historical evidence supports the resurrection of Jesus Christ? Why do I believe Jesus rose from the dead?

The Way Jesus Died

One argument against the resurrection suggests Jesus didn't really die on the cross. He only appeared to be dead, but He was actually unconscious due to His pain, shock, and loss of blood. Jesus was taken down from the cross and placed in Joseph's tomb, where He later revived and somehow managed to escape. This argument is called the "Swoon Theory."

The Bible says Jesus died on the cross (1 Cor. 15:3-4; Phil. 2:8). What do we know about crucifixions?

- **No one survived crucifixion:** Roman soldiers were professional executioners. Once a person was nailed to a cross, they died.

- **Scourging:** Jesus was scourged before He was nailed to the cross (Matt. 27:26). When the Romans scourged a victim, they would strip his clothing from his back and tie his arms around a post. This would stretch the flesh of his back, which would be beaten with a whip consisting of leather cords with metal beads or bones woven into the ends. Such a beating would reduce the victim's back to a tangled mass of flesh. Sometimes, the victims would actually die from the scourging before they could be crucified.

- **Couldn't carry His cross:** Simon of Cyrene (Matt. 27:32) was forced to carry Jesus' cross, which has always been understood as an indication that Jesus wasn't strong enough to do so.

- **Nailed to the cross:** The victim was thrown to the ground upon the cross, his arms would be stretched out, and large metal spikes would be nailed through his wrists. These nails would crush the median nerve, which would cause excruciating pain (the English word "excruciating" literally means "out of the cross"). The crossbeam would then be lifted and attached to the post. Another spike would be nailed through the victim's feet.

- **Dislocated shoulders:** The weight of the body on the outstretched arms would've dislocated both shoulders (Psalm 22:14).

- **Death by asphyxiation:** "Crucifixion is essentially an agonizingly slow death by asphyxiation. The reason is that the stresses on the muscles and diaphragm put the chest into the inhaled position; basically, in order to exhale, the individual must push up on his feet so the tension on the muscles would be eased for a moment. In doing so, the nail would tear through the foot, eventually locking against the tarsal bones. After managing to exhale, the person would then be able to relax down and take another breath in. Again, he'd have to push himself up to exhale, scraping his bloodied back against the coarse wood of the cross. This would go on and on until complete exhaustion would take over, and the person wouldn't be able to push up and breathe anymore" (Strobel, 198).

- **Side pierced:** Jesus died before the soldiers expected. To make sure Jesus was dead, a soldier pierced his side with a spear (John 19:31-34). John saw blood and water come forth from the wound, and Jesus later acknowledged that His hands bore the scars of nails and His side was pierced (John 20:25-27).

- **Pilate confirmed His death:** Joseph of Arimathea asked Pilate if he could bury Jesus' body (Mark 15:43-45). When Pilate received word from the centurion that Jesus was actually dead, he granted Joseph permission to take the body.

When we consider the things Jesus went through prior to and during His crucifixion, there's no way He could've survived the cross. He didn't pass out—He died!

> "But when they came to Jesus and saw that He was **already dead**, they did not break His legs. But one of the soldiers **pierced His side** with a spear, and immediately blood and water came out. "
>
> - John 19:33-34

QUESTIONS

1. Describe the "Swoon Theory" in your own words. _____

   _____

   _____

2. What was done to Jesus before He was crucified (Matt. 27:26)? _____

   _____

3. Describe what took place in a Roman scourging. You may want to look this up and provide some details that weren't mentioned in the lesson.

_____

_____

4. How do we know Jesus was actually nailed to a cross (John 20:25-27)?

_____

5. How did the soldier confirm Jesus was dead (John 19:33-34)? _____

_____

6. How did Pilate make sure Jesus was dead (Mark 15:44-45)? _____

_____

_____

The Way Jesus Was Buried

Some skeptics deny that Jesus was actually buried. As a rule, victims of crucifixion weren't given burials. The bodies of most crucified people were left to rot on the cross or were taken down and thrown away. However, archaeologists have discovered the remains of a crucified man with the nail still through his heel, so there were exceptions to this "rule."

We know Jesus was buried in haste, because He died on the Preparation Day. However, His body wasn't just thrown into a tomb and covered with a sheet. Jesus was buried according to "the custom of the Jews" (John 19:38-42).

In a Jewish burial, the body would've been wrapped with linen three times. First, the body would be wrapped to the armpits. Then, the arms would be placed at the side of the body, and the body would be wrapped again to the neck. Finally, the entire body would be wrapped.

Nicodemus helped Joseph bury Jesus. He brought a hundred pounds of myrrh and aloes. This mixture of spices would be mixed in with these layers of linen. Myrrh has the consistency of a gummy adhesive. Thus, these layers of linen would have been "glued" into place.

It would be impossible for a strong and healthy man to wrestle himself out of such an encasement, much less someone who has endured a Roman scourging and crucifixion.

QUESTIONS

7. Name the two men who buried Jesus (John 19:38-39)._____

    _____

8. In your own words, describe the way Jesus' body would've been prepared for burial._____

    _____

    _____

9. Do you think a normal man could free himself from such an encasement?_____

The Empty Tomb

What are the facts regarding the tomb in which the Lord was buried (Matt. 27:59-28:8)?

*   Jesus was buried in a new tomb (27:60). Jesus' body was the only body in the tomb, so His body wasn't mistaken for the body of another person.

*   This tomb was hewn out of rock. It was like a cave. It had no "back door" or second entrance.

*   The enemies of Jesus tried their best to keep the body of Jesus in the tomb.

*   A large stone was rolled against the door of the tomb, a seal was placed on the stone, and a guard was posted to keep the tomb from being disturbed.

Despite these facts and the efforts of the chief priests and Pharisees, the women found an empty tomb. What happened to the body?

We know the women didn't go to the wrong tomb. They'd gone to the tomb when Jesus was buried, and would've remembered where it was located (Matt. 27:61).

We know Jesus didn't survive to walk out of the tomb under His own power. Physically, He was in no condition to wrestle Himself out of the encasement of His burial cloth and push away the stone over the door of the tomb. Also, He would've needed to move the stone and sneak past the guards who were posted to keep His body in the tomb.

We know the disciples didn't steal the body. First of all, they weren't in a frame of mind to do so. They believed Jesus was dead and gone forever. Second, they couldn't have gotten past the guards to steal Jesus' body even if they'd wanted to.

We know the enemies of Jesus didn't steal His body. It was in their best interest for the body of Jesus to stay in the tomb.

The only possible explanation is that Jesus miraculously rose from the dead, as He said He would.

QUESTIONS

10. Let's say you're a detective. What facts could you learn from Joseph of Arimathea and Mary Magdalene concerning the tomb in which Jesus was buried (Matt. 27:60-61)? _____

_____

_____

11. What effort did the chief priests and the Pharisees put forth to keep the body of Jesus in the tomb (Matt. 27:65-66)?_____

_____

12. Let's say you're a lawyer building a case in favor of the Lord's resurrection. How would you answer the following arguments?
The women went to the wrong tomb._____

_____

_____

Jesus snuck out of the tomb. _____

_____

_____

The disciples took the body of Jesus out of the tomb and later claimed He rose from the dead._____

_____

_____

The chief priests and Pharisees took the body of Jesus from the tomb.

_____

_____

Conclusion

The Bible builds a strong case in favor of the resurrection of Jesus from the dead. We know Jesus actually died on the cross. We know Jesus was buried, and we know how He was buried. We know the empty tomb can't be explained by any natural causes. All of this evidence points to the validity of the resurrection of Jesus from the dead.

In our next lesson, we'll consider more evidence supporting the resurrection of Jesus. We'll also discuss the significance of His resurrection.

QUESTIONS

13. Why do you believe it is important that we be able to prove that Jesus rose from the dead? _____

_____

_____

_____

_____

14. Do you believe it is possible for a person to survive the things that happened to Jesus before and during His crucifixion? _____

_____

References

Moyer, Doy, _Standing on Solid Ground_, Russellville, AL, Norris Book Company, 1995, print

Strobel, Lee, _The Case For Christ_, Grand Rapids, MI, Zondervan Publishing House, 1998, print

Why I Believe Jesus Rose from the Dead (Part 2)

In this lesson, we'll continue our study of the evidence that supports the resurrection of Jesus from the dead.

The Post-Resurrection Appearances

Anyone can claim that someone has risen from the dead, but few people are likely to believe such a claim without evidence. The best evidence is "eyewitness" testimony.

After Jesus rose from the dead, He appeared to a number of people on several different occasions. Sometimes, He appeared to individuals, and sometimes to groups of people. Sometimes, it was outdoors; sometimes, it was indoors. On one occasion, Jesus ate with His disciples and encouraged them to touch Him (Luke 24:39-43), thus proving they weren't seeing a ghost but a real, living, flesh-and-blood person.

Thomas stands in the place of every skeptic alive today. When he heard the news that Jesus had risen from the dead, he stated, "Unless I see in His hands the print of the nails, and put my finger into the print of the nails, and put my hand into His side, I will not believe" (John 20:25). We sometimes refer to this disciple as "Doubting Thomas" because of his refusal to believe Jesus had risen from the dead. However, "Doubting Thomas" actually does mankind a great favor. He was skeptical of the resurrection and refused to believe without evidence. Notice what happened to Thomas:

"And after eight days, His disciples were again inside, and Thomas with them. Jesus came, the doors being shut, and stood in the midst, and

Key Passage

"To whom He also presented Himself **alive** after His suffering by many **infallible proofs**, being seen by them during forty days and speaking of the things pertaining to the kingdom of God."

- Acts 1:3

> "...He was seen by **Cephas**, then by **the twelve**. After that He was seen by over **five hundred brethren** at once, of whom the greater part remain to the present, but some have fallen asleep. After that He was seen by **James**, then by **all the apostles**. Then last of all **He was seen by me also**, as by one born out of due time."
>
> - 1 Corinthians 15:5-8

said, 'Peace to you!' Then He said to Thomas, 'Reach your finger here, and look at My hands; and reach your hand here, and put it into My side. Do not be unbelieving, but believing.' And Thomas answered and said to Him, 'My Lord and my God!' Jesus said to him, 'Thomas, because you have seen Me, you have believed. Blessed are those who have not seen and yet have believed.'" (John 20:26-29)

Thomas changed his mind. He saw the evidence he needed and believed that Jesus had risen from the dead. Thomas stands in the place of every honest skeptic who would follow him. Because of his demand for evidence, we can believe in the resurrection with even greater confidence.

In 1 Corinthians 15:5-8, the apostle Paul provides a list of individuals who saw the resurrected Christ. In addition to the apostles, Jesus was seen by over five hundred people at one time. Concerning this large group of eyewitnesses, Paul said "the greater part remain to the present" (v. 6). In this statement, Paul was welcoming the Corinthians' investigation into the validity of the Lord's resurrection. These eyewitnesses could be asked what they saw. Paul wouldn't make a statement like this if these individuals weren't willing to support the fact that Jesus had risen from the dead.

The Bible says the truth shall be determined by the testimony of two to three witnesses. "...On the evidence of two or three witnesses a matter shall be confirmed" (Deut. 19:15, NASB). There were over five hundred witnesses of the resurrected Christ. The validity of this fact has been more than confirmed!

QUESTIONS

1. What are some of the "infallible proofs" Jesus showed to prove He'd risen from the dead (Luke 24:39-43)? _____

    _____

    _____

2. How did Thomas react to the news of the Lord's resurrection (John 20:25)? _____

    _____

3. Did Thomas see the evidence he needed? _____

4. Explain how "Doubting Thomas" helps those who are skeptical of the Lord's resurrection today. _____

    _____

    _____

5. According to Deuteronomy 19:15, how many eyewitnesses are needed to establish a fact?_____

6. According to 1 Corinthians 15:6, how many people witnessed the resurrected Christ?_____

Circumstantial Evidence

Sometimes, a strong case is built, not on eyewitness testimony, but on what's called "circumstantial evidence." There are several things in the New Testament that point to the certainty of the resurrection of Jesus.

1. **The bravery of the disciples**
    When Jesus was arrested, His disciples fled in fear, and Peter later denied Him (Mark 14:50, 66-72). After the resurrection, these same men boldly preached the gospel in the face of opposition, threats, persecution, and even death. Men will not die for what they know to be a lie. The resurrection of Christ gave these men great confidence in their work.

2. **The beginning place of the church**
    The apostles didn't travel to some far off place to start preaching the resurrection of Jesus from the dead. The first gospel sermon was preached in the same city as the Lord's empty tomb (Acts 2). If the resurrection was a hoax, the gospel of Christ would've been easily exposed by the Jewish leaders.

3. **The conversion of skeptics**
    Thomas changed from doubter to believer (John 20:24-29). James, the brother of the Lord, was not a believer (John 7:5), but he went on to become one of the leading men of the church in Jerusalem (Gal. 1:18-19).

Saul of Tarsus was a great persecutor of the Lord's church (Acts 22:4-5; Gal. 1:13). However, much to the surprise of many disciples, Saul became the beloved apostle Paul (Acts 9:20-21). Why would a man who had such a promising future in Judaism turn his back on the training he'd received since childhood? The conversion of Saul is something Jews can't explain to this day. However, we know the reason he changed. He saw the risen Lord (Acts 26:9-20).

4. The first day of the week

The church was originally made up of Jewish converts who, for centuries, had kept the Sabbath (Saturday, the seventh day of the week; Ex. 20:8-11). However, there's a different day that was kept by the disciples in the early church: the first day of the week (1 Cor. 16:1-2; Acts 20:7). This happens to be the day on which Jesus rose from the dead (Matt. 28:1).

While none of these items take the place of eyewitness testimony, they strongly support the validity of the resurrection of Jesus from the dead.

QUESTIONS

7. Explain how the bravery of the apostles supports the validity of the Lord's resurrection._____

_____

_____

8. Why would it have been difficult to establish the church in Jerusalem if the Lord hadn't risen from the dead?_____

_____

9. Why did Saul of Tarsus become a follower of Christ?_____

_____

_____

10. Why do you think the early church met on the first day of the week as opposed to the Sabbath (Matt. 28:1)?_____

_____

_____

The Significance of the Resurrection

What makes the resurrection of Jesus Christ from the dead so important? Why should we care about whether or not we can prove Jesus actually rose from the dead?

1. **It proves Jesus is the Son of God.** The resurrection is the means by which God declared Jesus to be His Son (Rom. 1:4). It is also the means by which Jesus declared Himself to be the Son of God. He predicted His resurrection fifteen times in the gospel accounts.

2. **It validates our faith.** It's been said that Christianity either stands or falls with the resurrection. This is the point made by Paul in 1 Corinthians 15:12-19. According to this passage, if Jesus wasn't raised from the dead:

   - All gospel preaching is meaningless (v. 14).
   - Our faith is worthless (v. 14).
   - The apostles were liars (v. 15).
   - We're still in our sins (v. 17).
   - Those who have died have perished (v. 18).
   - Christians are to be pitied (v. 19).

3. **It assures us of future judgment.** "Truly, these times of ignorance God overlooked, but now commands all men everywhere to repent, because He has appointed a day on which He will judge the world in righteousness by the Man whom He has ordained. He has given assurance of this to all by raising Him from the dead" (Acts 17:30-31). The resurrection of Jesus from the dead is the assurance of our own resurrection and judgment.

QUESTIONS

11. How did God declare that Jesus was His Son (Rom. 1:4)?_____

_____

_____

12. Explain some of the consequences of believing Jesus didn't rise from

the dead (1 Cor. 15:12-19)?_____

_____

_____

13. How can we know we'll have to face the Lord in judgment (Acts 17:30-31)? _____

_____

_____

Conclusion

The resurrection of Jesus from the dead is the crowning piece of evidence in our faith. It gives meaning to everything we believe, teach, and practice. There may be questions with which we struggle throughout our entire lives, but without a risen Savior, our entire religion is empty and worthless.

Either Jesus rose from the dead as He said He would, or He and His apostles successfully carried out the greatest hoax in human history. If He didn't rise from the dead, we can ignore everything the Bible has to say, for it's based on a lie. However, if He did rise from the dead, we know we'll face Him in judgment after this life is over, and we also know He has the power to forgive us of our sins and grant us eternal life.

As with every other subject we've addressed in this workbook, there's solid evidence supporting the fact that Jesus Christ rose from the dead. What do you believe?

QUESTIONS

14. As we close this study, say you are a lawyer and you are building a case to prove that Jesus rose from the dead. What pieces of evidence would you use to make your case? Explain why you would use them? _____

_____

_____

_____

_____

_____

15. Are you ready to use the evidence you have gained in these thirteen lessons to help you "give a defense to everyone who asks you a reason for the hope that is in you" (1 Pet. 3:15)? _____

Closing Thoughts

This workbook has been an introduction to the study of evidences. It's my hope that each student will develop an interest in this subject and will continue to study evidences.

The following books are ones I've found to be helpful in my study of evidences. Please understand that, while I've found these books to be helpful and recommend them to others, I do not agree with everything said in each one of these books. Young people need to learn to be discerning readers, always testing what they read with the truth found in God's word.

- *Out with Doubt* by Kyle Butt, published by Apologetics Press, Inc.
- *Unraveling Evolution* by Joshua Gurtler, published by the Guardian of Truth Foundation
- *Introduction to Christian Evidences* by Ferrell Jenkins, published by the Guardian of Truth Foundation
- *Standing on Solid Ground* by Doy Moyer, published by Norris Book Company
- *The Bible on Trial* by Wayne Jackson, published by Christian Courier Publications
- *Defeating Darwinism* by Phillip E. Johnson, published by InterVarsity Press
- *The Battle for the Beginning* by John MacArthur, published by W Publishing Group
- *The Case for Faith* by Lee Strobel, published by Zondervan Publishing House
- *The Case for Christ* by Lee Strobel, published by Zondervan Publishing House

The following websites are also helpful, but one must practice discernment when reading the material found at these sites.

- "Answers in Genesis" – Evangelically-based apologetics organization founded by Ken Ham (www.AnswersinGenesis.org)
- "The Institute for Creation Research" – Evangelically-based apologetics organization founded by Dr. Henry Morris (www.icr.org)
- "Apologetics Press" (www.ApologeticsPress.com)
- "Creation Wiki" – Wikipedia-type website for creation material (www.CreationWiki.org)

Made in USA - Kendallville, IN